THE SELECTED POETRY OF BOHDAN RUBCHAK

SONGS OF LOVE, SONGS OF DEATH, SONGS OF THE MOON

THE SELECTED POETRY OF BOHDAN RUBCHAK:
SONGS OF LOVE, SONGS OF DEATH, SONGS OF THE MOON

by Bohdan Rubchak

Translated by Michael M. Naydan and Svitlana Budzhak-Jones
(with one translation by Liliana M. Naydan)

with:
a biocritical afterword by Marian J. Rubchak
a translator's afterword by Svitlana Budzhak-Jones
an essay on the poet by Mykola Riabchuk
a concise biography and timeline by Michael M. Naydan

Edited by Michael M. Naydan

Publishers Maxim Hodak & Max Mendor

© 2020, Michael M. Naydan,
Svitlana Budzhak-Jones, and Liliana M. Naydan

© 2020, Glagoslav Publications

www.glagoslav.com

ISBN: 978-1-912894-84-0

First published in English by Glagoslav Publications in August 31, 2020

A catalogue record for this book is available from the British Library.

This book is in copyright. No part of this publication may be reproduced, stored in a retrieval system or transmitted in any form or by any means without the prior permission in writing of the publisher, nor be otherwise circulated in any form of binding or cover other than that in which it is published without a similar condition, including this condition, being imposed on the subsequent purchaser.

THE SELECTED POETRY OF BOHDAN RUBCHAK

SONGS OF LOVE, SONGS OF DEATH, SONGS OF THE MOON

BY BOHDAN RUBCHAK

Translated by
Michael M. Naydan and Svitlana Budzhak-Jones
(with one translation by Liliana M. Naydan)

GLAGOSLAV PUBLICATIONS

CONTENTS

ACKNOWLEDGEMENTS 9
PREFACE 11

from the collection *THE STONE GARDEN* (1956) 13
    IN A ROOM OF A HUNDRED MIRRORS 14
    AUTUMN 15
    THE LIPS OF LEAVES 16
    THE GRAVES OF MY GREAT
    GRANDSONS WERE HERE 17
    TO HAMLET 18
    NOCTURNAL MINIATURES 19
    MIDNIGHT IMPROVISATION 21
    ARS POETICA 22
    FROM *THE SONG OF SONGS* 23

from the collection *THE RADIANT BETRAYAL* (1960) 27
    THE RADIANT BETRAYAL 28
    FOR FRANCESCA 29
    FOR FRANCESCA AGAIN 30
    THE ANGEL'S BETRAYAL 31
    NOVEMBER 32
    DECEMBER 33
    A RECOLLECTION OF THE MOON 34
    THE WING OF ICARUS 40

BE SILENT 42

from the collection *TO THE GIRL WITHOUT A COUNTRY* (1963) . 43
    TO THE GIRL WITHOUT A COUNTRY 44
    AND THEN WE RODE HOME 45
    A SLEEPLESS NIGHT 46
    FROM GOTTFRIED BENN 47
    THE DANCER 48
    SONG OF A WOMAN BENEATH THE MOON 49
    IN THE LAST HOUSE OF THE MIRROR 50
    ABSENCE 51
    THREE EMBLEMS 52
    THE FARNESS OF ROADS 54
    A WINDY ICARUS 55
    A RESTLESS SLEEP 56
    THE DESTINATION 57
    AN AUTUMN DAY 58

from the collection *A PERSONAL CLIO* (1967) 59
    AUTUMN ROMANCE 60
    TO CLIO 62
    THREE FRAGMENTS OF "THE WORD" 63
    A STONE 64
    DON JUAN 65
    MOZART 67
    CHOPIN 68
    A SMALL POET 70
    MY ITHACA 71
    A WINTRY ROMANCE 72
    A SONG FOR MARIANA 73

NOTES FROM A DIARY 74
    1. THE FIRST POEM 74
    2. OUTSIDE THE WINDOW 74
    3. A JUSTIFICATION 75
    4. SEVERAL OBSERVATIONS 76
DESTINATION 78

from the collection *DROWNING MARENA* (1983) 79
    DROWNING MARENA 80
    LETTER TO HOME 82
    A BOOK FROM HOME 83
    DECADENCE 84
    A FLASH AND A REFLECTION 85
    A MANDARIN FOR MY WIFE 86
    THE FEMALE SAINT AND THE DEVIL 87
    SKETCHES 88
        1. A MADRIGAL 88
        2. COMPLAINING ABOUT DECEMBER 89
    THE GODS 90

from the collection *THE WING OF ICARUS* (1983; 1991) 91
    THE BLACKSMITH 92
    RAIN 93
    AN EVENING PRAYER 94
    NARCISSUS 95
    THE HARDEST GAME 96
    DRAMATURGY 97
    COMPRESSIONS 98

AFTERWORD I
MY LIFE WITH THE POET AND HIS POETRY
by Marian J. Rubchak 103

AFTERWORD II
THE COMPLEXITY AND PERPLEXITY OF BOHDAN RUBCHAK:
REMARKS ON TRANSLATING HIS POETRY
by Svitlana Budzhak-Jones 136

AFTERWORD III
THE STIGMATA OF WINGS: ON THE POETRY OF BOHDAN RUBCHAK
by Mykola Riabchuk (Translated by Michael M. Naydan) 152

AFTERWORD IV
BOHDAN RUBCHAK (1935-2018): A CONCISE BIOGRAPHY
by Michael M. Naydan 158

AFTERWORD V
TIMELINE OF BOHDAN RUBCHAK (1935-2018) 163

AFTERWORD VI
PAGE NUMBERS OF PUBLICATIONS
WHERE POEMS FIRST APPEARED 167

ACKNOWLEDGEMENTS

This volume would not have been possible without the enormous support and efforts of Marian J. Rubchak, who also goes by Mariana or Mar'iana in Ukrainian, to whom we are exceedingly grateful. She went far beyond the call of duty to promote the legacy of her husband Bohdan Rubchak and devoted an enormous amount of time to explaining biographical connections in his poetry.

The poems "Dramaturgy" and "The Angel's Betrayal" both first appeared in the poetry anthology *A Hundred Years of Youth* (Litopys Publishers, 2000). All other translations are appearing here for the first time. Mykola Riabchuk's essay "The Stigmata of Wings: On the Poetry of Bohdan Rubchak" first appeared in Ukrainian as a preface to Rubchak's final collection *Krylo Ikarove* (The Wing of Icarus; Kyiv: Dnipro Publishers, 1991). We are grateful to Alina Zhurbenko for her assistance in the final stages of the project.

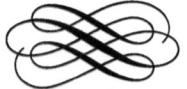

PREFACE

BY MICHAEL M. NAYDAN

Prior to the appearance of this collection only a handful of Bohdan Rubchak's poems have appeared in English translation. This volume attempts to remedy that situation for a truly outstanding Ukrainian poet in the North American diaspora, Bohdan Rubchak, who died in 2018 at the age of 83. Rubchak was a child of the displaced post-war generation that escaped from the traumas of World War II to find a new life in a new land on the other side of the Atlantic Ocean. Bohdan, whom I had met on numerous occasions, had a playfully abrasive personality with a biting sense of humor that immediately set him off from the crowd. To compare him to a poet from the English poetry tradition, one whose poetry he knew quite intimately, I would say that he reminds me a bit of the character and poetry of Dylan Thomas with a similarly obsessive raging against the idea of the dying of the light. Bohdan took Thomas's advice and never went gentle into that good night.

Bohdan's complex, at times seemingly impenetrable poetry, which makes the translator's task imposing, is filled with meaning on multiple levels – semantic, syntactic, auditory, symbolic, allusive, and in other innovative ways, which Svitlana Budhak-Jones illuminates in detail in her essay in an afterword to this volume.

It has been a great pleasure for me to work with Svitlana on these English translations to unravel the mysteries of Rubchak's poetry. She contributed her expansive linguistic expertise in both Ukrainian and English as well as her cultural knowledge of her native Ukraine to our translations. This volume of selected works comprises: 1) translations from many of the best poems of all six of Rubchak's published collections; 2) Mariana Rubchak's revelatory biocritical essay "My Life with Bohdan Rubchak and His Poetry," which includes numerous observations from her husband's soon to be deposited archival materials; 3) Svitlana Budzhak-Jones's essay "The Complexity and Perplexity of Bohdan Rubchak: Remarks on Translating His

Poetry"; 4) a translation of the first half of Ukrainian writer and literary critic Mykola Riabchuk's essay "The Stigmata of Wings: On the Poetry of Bohdan Rubchak"; a concise biography of Bohdan by me, checked by Mariana, which corrects various errors that persist in Internet and other published articles; and a timeline also corrected by her.

The poems listed in Afterword VI contain page numbers in parentheses from the 1991 *Krylo Ikarove* (The Wing of Icarus) selected works edition, the poet's final and definitive collection, which, according to Mariana, the poet corrected meticulously. Poems that were included in this volume that come from original volumes that did not appear in that selected works edition are marked with a page number and an asterisk to indicate that the source is from the original collections. This is done to facilitate ease of reference for those who wish to compare the translations to the originals.

FROM THE COLLECTION
THE STONE GARDEN (1956)

IN A ROOM OF A HUNDRED MIRRORS

In a room of a hundred mirrors, I, self-loving,
see myself beautifully distorted. And only
in the gray garden of stone walls – on their surface –
my reflection can never betray me.

I often wear grand clothes. They
glitter on me rich in colors
on the miniature stage of my intimate theater.
But in bare

white light – between the bushes of the stone garden –
my clothing turns entirely gray, my fairy-tale mask grows pale,
the makeup of the grotesque runs, and I
become myself again.

October 1955

AUTUMN

A Byzantine cathedral – this autumn is.

Icons of the evangelists on its Royal Doors,
In deep, contemplative colors,
Framed in time-worn gold,
Forged into grape vines.

It seems – the rings of the glow like chalices of salvation
(Birth. Yes. Not a demise) –
Emerged through the mosaics of windows,
Through trembling depictions of martyrs.

And it seems the trees that have become wise –
Are a band of Christ's disciples.

January 1955

* * *

The lips of leaves, somewhere nearby, call out to me –
Bohdan! They faintly beseech.
Like a lover they invite, the lips of leaves implore.

I can't come – I'm a son of the city,
I'm a son of gray sky, not the blue sky of spring;
My day and my sleep are factory whistles.

I see spring,
because a patch of snow and soot between stone walls
became slightly smaller,

but I know spring,
for somewhere the lips of leaves confess to the sun;
and there somewhere it seems
the miracle of forgotten gods
rises and unsteadily grows.

March 1955

* * *

The graves of my great grandsons were here,
Where you and I, my sweetheart, lie,
And to you I am – your young lover.

In the deep blue twilights of the middle ages
I showed my beloved the grass:
It grows from the children of my children.

March 1955

TO HAMLET

Not the first of books, and not the last,
and not the sagacity of a dry historian –
the skull of old Yorick
will answer all these questions.

Everything will be quite simple:
in sleep unable to overcome fatigue
you'll find a long familiar
treasure made of yellow bone.

In the morning you'll suddenly rise from bed,
having forgotten your losses forever:
because its dreadful smile
will teach you how to live and how to die.

NOCTURNAL MINIATURES
(Imitations of Haiku)

1.
(PEOPLE)

My small skiff
sails past others:
    between us is the abyss.

2.
(STARS)

I opened a book
of always new poems:
    I read the stars.

3.
(THE MOON)

A forlorn night wears
The medallion of her lover
    Who fell in battle yesterday.

4.
(LOVE)

Two ripe cherries
On an azure palm:
    My love and I.

5.
(A CLOUDLET)

Instead of carp
A cloudlet was caught
    In thick nets.

6.
(A LAKE)

The moon's glow
Creates a miracle on the water:
    A road made of pearls.

7.
(A GIRL)

Black hair
Became adorned in spring
    By a cherry blossom.

MIDNIGHT IMPROVISATION

1.
You'll knock on the door;
sharp footsteps along the littered floorboards,
and a face – a green spot in the darkness:
My mother's ill. Don't come in.

2.
The sky clenched you into a fist. It's clammy.
Warm humidity chokes you. You walk. By the pavement
the black-branched stubbornness of an ailing tree is surprising.
The toothless roar of black windows knows
you're imprisoned and the lantern watchman keeps walking behind you.

3.
Which door is it I knock on? Who'll receive me? Who'll
understand that your body is a ship,
that your body –
is a caravel, sunken to the bottom of some sea, with fish
kissing it, starfish, polyps touching it?

4.
You'll feel Tomorrow on your lips like a kiss.
And the wind tomorrow will carry scraps of friezes
of hours, zephyr will carry off frag-
                                    ments of friezes
                                                      hours,
zephyr will carry off sculptures of azure nothingness.
     And you will say:
               "I am."

Today, you're just a breath, sight, hearing – unarticulated,[1]
and your body – is a ship, drowned somewhere
                                            in some sea.

January 1956

---

[1] In the original publication of *Kaminnyi sad* (The Stone Garden) this is "nevydymyi" (invisible).

ARS POETICA

To be mute, indifferent, as always the door is closed.
To be forgotten like an old statue in a small town.
To know just the love of a stone, the opaque heart of a stone,
and to see the world in black and white shadows.

There is too much green, too much carmine rose.
Blue-arched shadows mercilessly embraced you.
There are too many nuances: love, desire, suffering –
they cloaked their lives with the murk of sadness and delight.

To search only for the essence, to search for just the horizon of being –
the essence of being. To feel space: the flight of black birds far off,
to sense time: distinct drawings in black caves,
and with an absolute wind to understand your day, poet.

March 1956

FROM *THE SONG OF SONGS*

* * *

Come down with me from Lebanon, my friend,
Go with me from Lebanon!
Make haste from the top of Amana,
from the top of Shenir and Hermon,
from the lions' dens,
from the mountains where there are lynx.[2]

Come with me.

Give me your hand.
We spoke too much about eternity.
Give me your hand,
we know passion
only from the paintings of Tintoretto.[3]

Let us go together:
perhaps we'll find the path
from this stone garden.

* * *

Yesterday a peculiar gentleman
with a beard
wearing a pince-nez came up to me,
            an ichthyosaurus from the last century:

---

[2]   Rubchak cites this passage from the Ukrainian-Ruthenian Bible of 1906 in Panteleimon Kulish's translation, which was republished in London in 1947 by The British and Foreign Bible Society. It differs slightly from Old Church Slavonic and other Ukrainian Bibles as well as from the New King James Version of the Songs of Solomon 4:8, which follows: "8 Come with me from Lebanon, my spouse, With me from Lebanon. Look from the top of Amana, From the top of Senir and Hermon, From the lions' dens, From the mountains of the leopards."
We have opted for the literal translation here from the version Rubchak quotes.

[3]   Venetian expressionist painter Jacopo Tintoretto (ca. 1518-1594) known mostly for his large canvases, muscular figures, and bold strokes.

"Wissen Sie,
In dem Tiergarten hat man alle Tiere getötet."⁴

Give me your hand.

I met a young man recently.
He wanted to talk to someone
about the heat burning out his brain cells.

He said to me
(speaking fast, choking in pain)
"On the other side, after passing through rain,
there stands a little bridge where the roads meet.
I walk there every day, my friend,
to look for my little tin soldier."

Let us go,
perhaps we will find the path.

    * * *

*King Solomon
built for himself a palaquin
made of wood from Lebanon.
Little silver columns,
gold handrails,
seating of purple cloth,
the entire inside tidied up with love
of the daughters of Jerusalem.*⁵

Pain glitters on nerves,
like dew on a spider web.

---

⁴ In German: "You know, All the animals in the zoo were killed."

⁵ The quote is from the Songs of Solomon 3:9-10 and in the New King James Version would be: "9 Of the wood of Lebanon Solomon the King Made himself a palanquin: 10 He made its pillars of silver, Its support of gold, Its seat of purple, Its interior paved with love By the daughters of Jerusalem." We've opted again for a literal version of the Kulish Ukrainian translation of the Bible that Rubchak used.

Barcarolles of porches, jasmine bushes, quiet
                              whispers –

coarse novels –
tear the baby apart prematurely
into a thousand little trembling dwarfs.

Oh, well, Thomas Buddenbrook,[6]
It's hard to hang forever,
like a bridge, between two distant shores.

   * * *

And again a meeting:
A paranoid guy comes up close to me.
Neon lights glow in his eyes,
                  a mambo twitching on his face.

What will he say to me?

He passes next to me
repeating [in English] monotonously:

"This is the last stop,
as far as we go!
This is the last stop,
as far as we go!"

Give me your hand, my love,
let us go away from here.
Let us go search for
other words, for other gardens[7] near.

---

[6] One of the protagonists of Thomas Mann's 1901 novel *Buddenbrooks* (Buddenbrooks: Verfall einer Familie) about the decline of a wealthy merchant family over three generations.

[7] "Sad" can also be translated as "orchard." We've opted for "garden" in the translation because of our sense of Rubchak's meaning as a kind of walled-off English garden with trees as well as the notion of the paradisal biblical Eden.

FROM THE COLLECTION
THE RADIANT BETRAYAL (1960)

THE RADIANT BETRAYAL

You need more solitude
than the one in four walls:
you need to fall on your knees
inside of yourself forever.

You need so many farewells
with spring, with tenderness, with the world,
to touch the edge of sunrays
at least once with your icy age.

And you need to walk for so long
in unforgivingly bright rays,
and in the mute deserts of solitude
speak the shadows to yourself

and fall into the gloom of abysses
where the fruit and angel had fallen,
so that in the shadows that you sanctified,
the radiant betrayal would burst into bloom.

1960

FOR FRANCESCA

You conceal the apocalypse beneath your
eyelids. In my rib cage an unforgivable beast
is quieting down. An assemblage of pointy-blue stars
wants to burn out what's left of my brain.

Why are you here, why? Your worlds
have wilted beyond the point measured by Mondays;
to whom are you bringing offerings by the thousands –
voiceless, pointless ones – every night?

You attested to hundreds of deaths. Now
even the breast of the moon is rent by suffering
because an evil memory has shredded the possibility of dreams.

But still you continue to wait. Because sometimes
a fiery bird flies in and calls to you,
attesting to your lips with its wing.

FOR FRANCESCA AGAIN

The adorned hand of the mighty world
will tear up even our recollection of an image,
and something infinitely tender, something living
will wither, without waiting for a response.

In expectation you will touch a fresh branch,
but knowledge will no longer blow from it,
because a tree that's native and new
will become petrified into a stalagmite's cold.

Dreams, gardens, buildings, and towers
will depart, those who were friends will too –
melting in empty infinitude.

And before you even glance back, that's when
he will enter, on his clothes
bands of eternal mist will quiet down.

THE ANGEL'S BETRAYAL

Shoulders have grown weary from clumsy wings,
like the kind on old wood engravings.
In the corners of his mouth – the smile of a sybarite,
and on sandals – the pavement's dust.

Because he took the earth by the skyline,
the earth has taken too great of a toll:
the only truth of the myth is already concealed,
and there is no strength to imagine flight.

And though the world enticed you by the gifts of nights,
and even though the burden of things has chained you –
you will remain an uneasy stranger:

unwashed marks glisten in your eyes,
and the wings get in the way, and
the blinding recollection of that first azure burns.

– Translated by Liliana Naydan

NOVEMBER

To this day white-maned
steeds have lather in their blood,
to this day the sea speaks of another shore,
but already autumn has taken your cherry-like,
silky face into its dry palms.

To this day the nights whisper
about blistering meetings,
and a tree promises another meeting,
but already gestures become empty, and a white-lipped
recollection caresses the brow for the last time.

To this day equal to the stars
eyes rejoice in facets,
and another joy glows in mirrors of tears,
and there already is the frozen flight of a bird in your eyes:
there already is no pain in them at all.

DECEMBER

From the cold capital city of my eyes
I look at the land of the soft earth –
of sloping fields, strawberry forests,
and lustful rivers.

From the stone fortress of my being
I would want to depart through the gates of lips
onto an untrodden path – to bring a sign
to the villages of hearts.

To open the rough fence of my forehead
like the nocturnal silence of pan flutes,
and to come to them like a sable, a fox,
an owl, and a dream.

But I know: I will dress in a brocade cape
and will touch the gate with my ancestral ring –
then the frost will kill the blood of trees and
the green blood of grass.

A RECOLLECTION OF THE MOON
Fragments

* * *

When I touch your face, the tips of
my fingers open like apple blossoms,
and above us the moon
lives the life of a saint.

Then
an immaculate horizon
is born in me,
and you touch it
like a spring breeze.

But one day it will come,
the moon that used to be our friend –
and with a malevolent touch it will transform our joy
into dry sand,

but we'll still take two handfuls of it,
pouring it from one greedy hand to another,
in vain looking for that intimate miracle
that for so long
once was with us.

We'll still look together at the river reaches
and into the reaches of our hearts
until the cold consciousness
of the impotence of our efforts stabs us –
until we understand
that everything has already died for us.

Then we'll bid farewell
with an awkward, slightly bemused smile,
leaving one another –
like strangers.

* * *

Somewhere beyond suns are dreams,
and in them is the world of the moon.

* * *

Rounded memories hang
on branches of silence, ripening,
like plums. I know:
Ishtar has left you
and you're an empty garden
where white statues of solitude
resemble the whiteness of death.

* * *

Lips startled at a question.

* * *

No, it's not time yet –
in the most distant star, the diamond-like body of death still shines,
and the festive gestures of days like a living veil
screen the consciousness of your face's reflections
multiplied a thousand times. But remember: someday you'll see it again
                                                                  and again—

it will be framed by wilted roses, and your glance back
will turn into two pillars of salt – and your powerless gaze
will search for azure butterflies in vain.

* * *

When
mirrors will already be fading in my eyes,
when my palms' trees will be turning black –

when the last fruit will be falling from my forehead,
and autumn will be hanging gray adornments over my temples –

be with me then.

Be with me
when behind my eyes only
a large empty white moon remains –

and nothing more.

Love
me
then.

* * *

Be near and dear to me –
we'll step out to the furthest edges of being,
far beyond the cliffs, onto which waves of feelings
break apart –
to lands where expansive reaches
merge with the moon's glow,
where there is no movement, just the universe's eternal swaying,
where from each leaf –
from everything –
sap seeps into us giving us
total firmness,

where in the moon's glow
shadows of our past
fade away.

* * *

With your palms you'll lift up
the relics of the moon
to my lips.
I'll kiss them all over,
and they'll light up a white
fire in my soul.

It will become majestic:
all around
summer, winter, spring,

fall, summer, winter,
spring will fly by,
but it will keep burning.

And everything that touches it –
even moments –
will turn into cathedrals and trees.

* * *

The moon
with its shining
changes the world like the eyes of a child.

* * *

The moon – yes. The moon knows
even the branches, even the stones.

The light of the moon
does not know how to separate bodies
and it conceals
reveries and silent shadows,

the light of the moon
makes white marks,
and you enter
into a recollection from the furthest edges.

The light of the moon
doesn't know how to judge matters,
though it carves
the paths of fate on a palm,
the light of the moon
doesn't know how to separate bodies,
even though it knows
how to pierce foreheads with a sting.

The moon – yes. The moon knows.
The moon is – alpha. The moon is – omega.

* * *

Like the eyes of a child
the moon
discovers the kernels of things.

* * *

Give everything to the moon:
suffering and joy,
powerful love on the earth burnt by the sun,
a loaf of bread in hardworking hands,
a child's prayer,
the pregnancy of silence, the disquiet of song,
a calm look, the serenity of cemeteries,
the lakes and clouds –

give everything to the moon,
the cold moon.

* * *

The moon
trims the brows of cliffs,
in stone
it whispers out its dream,

and in stone,
images of the distant past are born.

* * *

Lonely girls
carry the stigmata of the moon on their breasts –
two reflections of its face
that fill with yearning pain at night –

that fill with uncontrollable thirst
and drink its fullness.

And then
in the golden reaches of their hair,
the full moon glows,
and their white bodies
are chambers for it.

* * *

Now comes what
you even feared to dream:
that radiance,
implacably white.

It's as if
the circle of the moon
flies uncontrollably
toward your face –

as if the moon
with its light penetrates –
even deeper, deeper, deeper
into your eyes.

* * *

The moon – yes. The moon knows.
The moon is – alpha. The moon is – omega.

THE WING OF ICARUS

1

A crystal first beginning arose on the sixth day.
There was a little boy: there was the world. Softsteppingly
he treaded across the new world. A seven-starred beast
sang the truth to him, the most immediate of all and wordless.
And the angel was still young.

A crystal first beginning arose on the sixth day.
A youngster. Guarded a wolf from evil. Gave a home to young deer.
The days ran up to him, running around him like children,
and the apple tree of flight blossomed all in white for him –
immaculately.

A crystal first beginning arose on the sixth day:
a man. He knew the universe. He mined his first word.
In him the marriage of the sun and sleepy serpents exploded
on dunes above the young sea. He wanted
to leave the mark of his good name in the wind.
To fly.

2

The crystal first beginning fell on the seventh day.
Evil poured all round. Torrents of gentle water tore out the earth.
Birds closed their mysterious faces to the sun,
the wind broke emblems of flight, and bushes came
to punish.

The crystal first beginning fell on the seventh day,
and the seventh day fell. There remained the night
to knot wings with the dreams of hot hands,
in a fury of sage grass, in the captivity of wormwood. The bushes
that had come closed up. Dark bushes.

The crystal first beginning fell on the seventh day:
the youth went to false priests, to blood merchants.
hiding his first desire deep in his eyes,
and that was it. The grandsons of fishermen found
the broken wing in the bushes.

BE SILENT

Be silent. Let lips smash myths,
and let them stop fighting with the shadow.
Over the entire earth poisonous flowers
of your blackest guilt have sprouted.

Now is not the time for azure-breasted birds
that you carried through a flood and pestilence,
for each bird is crushed by the structures
of monsters made by your hands.

Be silent. Let your lips burn with salt,
for your whisper will not move heavy glaciers.
Look: in your cellars old pages
of the wisest books have grown moldy.

The hand that used to caress punishes,
and sharp hail breaks grapevines.
You betrayed the world, your world is dying,
so turn your garden into a land of silence.

FROM THE COLLECTION
TO THE GIRL WITHOUT A COUNTRY (1963)

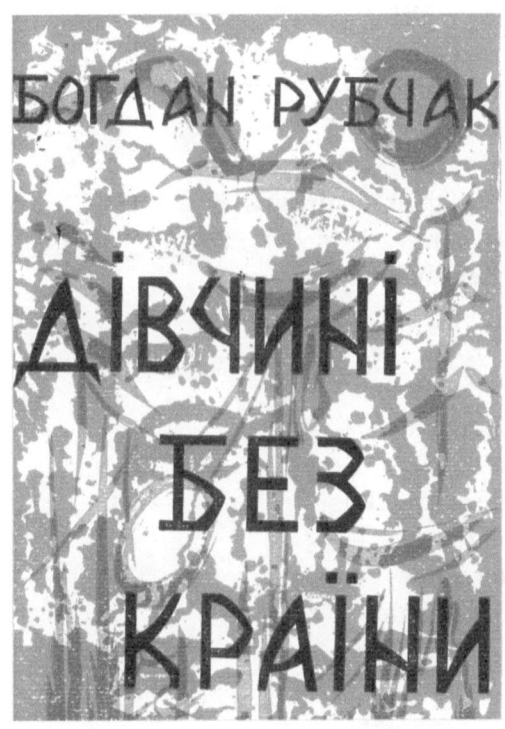

TO THE GIRL WITHOUT A COUNTRY

Good sister of birds,
girl without memory,
every night you watch
the singing of strangers through murkiness,
every morning you watch,
howling through golden weather,
the way in the workshops of hearts
winter is being made.

Forever unknown girl
without a constellation,
everywhere you watch
the saddest songs of eyes,
so clearly you see
eagles measuring their daydreams
and tearing out sons
from old mothers' hearts.

Girl without a road,
traveler without a home,
our noontides are pale,
clouded by pain.
What will you say about us
after your long journey,
when you enter alone
into your radiant home?

AND THEN WE RODE HOME

Recollections, teeming with pain,
swirl, nudge, knead,
as the rails turn white along the field,
shining with farewells of the moon.

My love is already sitting
before her daily mirror:
her face – the wound of love –
bandaged with anger.

And her eyes already are not workrooms
of suns, and hair – not crazy,
hands don't want to sing:
gloom becomes jaded through the train car.

Weary of myths lips
grew pale. We have no choice but to return.
The Non-believer – World-Birthgiver
caresses lamps at stations.

A SLEEPLESS NIGHT

The night conquered my dreams
with the blue sword of the moon.
On the white sails of memory
it spins your body.

Slyly it includes your eyes
in the unsolved game of stars,
in an empty home it deceives
with the hot touch of your hands.

Joy, rusty with despair,
shadows of vows and despondence,
it crowns them with a good memory
and prepares rigging for a poem,

so that it, like a moonstone,
in the murky darkness of the heart
would wear for ages instead of radiance
your intangible shadow.

FROM GOTTFRIED BENN

I'll send drowsiness to your eyes,
I'll leave a kiss on your lips,
and I'll myself carry the night, Angst,
and everything that's born in dreams.

I tenderly place onto your brow
both sadness and warm laughter.
Meanwhile the night, deadly cold,
will howl in my chest.

You are weak for the depths that are with us,
for those demands, for those imposts:
I'll send you kisses in the evenings –
and will rise up alone.

THE DANCER

Her body bends like a lily
with a soft breeze of sadness and pleasure.
A frothy fountain, like a tassel,
suddenly burst into laughter and grew hushed.

Arms are swimming in feelings.
They shine – the play of sparks.
Someone tears apart the heart
with mute farewells at night.

And happiness, warmly bid welcome,
rustles like incoming waves.
Look: a forlorn, joyful moment
began to stir its branches.

SONG OF A WOMAN BENEATH THE MOON

The moon wants to make love,
every night he calls out a song,
but his face is bewitched
by the night into stone.

The lad aroused by dreams,
in numb fury has stained
the bed of my merriment
with the foam of madness.

My day now is eyeless,
without his mother my son cries:
for the only world is the frenzied
moon, my intended.

He drinks my sleepwalking songs
in nightly revelry,
and the stone of his face
calls me to a dark bed.

1963

IN THE LAST HOUSE OF THE MIRROR

In the crystal thickets of a mirror
you will awaken your own beast
and from you it will tear off
the last face of the world.

On the naked sea of the mirror
you will lose the havens of time,
you will not find days, nights,
despair and hopes.

In the hot desert of the mirror
there will be no shade of a tree,
there will not even be respite
for your apparent loneliness.

ABSENCE

Final doors
will not let in fierce,
feathery beasts.

Boundless eyes
already will not begin to cry,
will not look twice.

The deadly sun
in vain burns
the barrenness of the heart.

THREE EMBLEMS

1. A VISTA AND A FACE

The high calling of a poplar tree
stretches its arms to the sky.
Stone harvests rumble
in the strands of thunder.

And a white recollection cries
over the black breaking off of a song:
eyes gone astray shine –
almonds of pain.

Suns and hearts of childhood buzz
on the pine needles of a downpour,
in order to resound
in a torrent of confessions, but

through the black branches of fingers,
into the wild gardens of these palms
like the fruit of the moon
your face fell.

2. IN THE LAST HOUSE OF THE MIRROR

In the crystal thicket of a mirror
you'll awaken your own beast,
and from you it will tear off
the final face of the world.

On the naked sea of the mirror
you'll lose harbors of time,
you'll find neither days, nor nights,
nor despair, nor hopes.

In the hot desert of the mirror
there will be no shade of a tree,
there will not even be sleep
for your placid loneliness.

3. ABSENCE

The terminal door
does not allow ferocious,
feathered beasts to enter.

Boundless eyes
already won't begin to cry,
they won't look twice.

The lethal sun
in vain burns
the desert of the heart.

THE FARNESS OF ROADS

Once again the paths of snowstorms,
once again bridges.
The windy tipsiness of youth
avenges with distance.

You've lost in the faces of seas,
in a sea of faces,
a ray that May had been saving
in the wings of a bee.

You've tossed into the clattering of roads
the whispers of miracles
woven on precious
needles of rain.

The bark of blood birches
no longer shines silver –
just the farness of losses does,
the farness of a star.

A WINDY ICARUS

A wing-eyed Icarus wants to plait out
dreams in the wind again,
and in him there's a warm-bodied river
out of which he can't swim.

> He raised his eyelashes toward warm lands
> and gushed into the wind in a whirl,
> forgetting about the verdict of blood
> in his perfidious faith.

He is destined to hang
in a dirty bureau like us –
yet the maniac took a fancy
for dreaming out what no one had achieved.

> Madman! Higher than a salvo!
> Not knowing the barbs of the wind,
> in its whistling he seeks tidings,
> as if that wind were prophetic.

For him life cannot be laid out
in white on black:
it's best – like everlasting torment –
to curse it out from your memory.

A RESTLESS SLEEP

In restless sleep, tell me, whom you were looking for?
Which peaceful day, whose hand?
Which azure blue, which beneficial herbs,
which God-given words that the years have not granted?

Brothers reach the crowns and the blackest depths,
they fly to plow the fields of the most distant worlds,
but you don't accept these prideful hours,
and your lips whisper: "That's not what I want from you."

Cities circulate in veins, bridges shake in your eyes,
mercilessly the grid of crossroads brands your brow,
and the entire tenderness of the world, which you have never caressed,
doesn't want to go away. It wounds with the blades of dreams. It hurts.

THE DESTINATION

Defiance is futile here –
the world won't say: "Return!"
Far from tomorrow and yesteryear
something on high will drive the boat.

Farewells, the sun, the circle
of infinity will burn:
the banner of your endurance
will be your only friend.

There will be no hugs of home,
with nowhere to come to.
You'll feel deadly exhaustion,
but you won't be able to come ashore.

AN AUTUMN DAY

This day is so autumn-like, like three days of sleet.
Like forgotten letters. Like a soldier's mother .

Like an untied slip of a shoe on a wet cobblestone.
Like an unfinished building being built.

Your farewell is quiet, akin to this day expiring.
Like a bird. Like the black question of a tree.

Like my poems. Like the autumn of a face.
Like the cold marks of the moon on a lake.

FROM THE COLLECTION
A PERSONAL CLIO (1967)

AUTUMN ROMANCE

1

When October sent withered leaves
onto the world
it killed March passion
and the myth of April

the crowns in my garden that are priceless
have faded away–
for the starry joy of your pupils
has withered

2

Many springs have passed,
many summers,
on eternal river reaches the chronicle of branches
writes changes;

The July thirst of blood smothered
with kisses is being squeezed
out from maple leaves again
by the bile of expiring

3

In search of shadows of the past,
of distant wonders,
this October I walked every day
to the autumn woods

to listen to the wind grieving
in the violas of branches,
whispering in response to thoughts
about the autumn of the world.

4

But in vain: a bee swarm
of phantoms scattered,
for a whirlwind blew specks of dreams
out of my eyes,

destroyed the nets of primeval spun yarn
and nests of birds,
and in flowers the starry joy
of your pupils.

TO CLIO[8]

All the same, you're just an hysterical spasm,
Clio. A downpour on stone slabs,
a momentary scorpion on stalactites –
the annals of absolute history.

Your monument, reviled, mourned,
will crumble into gravel for hundred-pawed trails.
The foliage and the corpses of insects will cover
the proud coat of arms, nurtured in winged blood.

In a kaleidoscope, sumptuous with gilding,
you will flash in several bright figures,
and then time, like snow crowning crosses on the mountains,
will crown the busts with ash-covered eternity.

Suits of armor, gonfalons, crowns
will become a nest of rats, a worm-eaten state,
and the mold of rusty indifference will raze
wounds of the host, the runes of victory.

Break the quill and sword on the cliff's epos,
deliver the epochs and robes to the moss museum,
for you will not defeat the encroaching ivy, the predatory
formations of thickets, not in battle or in their depiction.

---

[8] The Greek Muse and goddess of history. She is one of the nine daughters of Zeus who reside on Mount Parnassus.

THREE FRAGMENTS OF "THE WORD"

1

Needles of pikestaffs
crookedly fly.
From a cloud of patches
prophesying birds.

In black stalks
smoke cuts the horizon.
The evil birds
predatorily caw.

2

From the sun at dawn
the host sways.
Tents are burning,
helmets burn.

The sky is flaring,
pupils flare.
Shaggy foxes
choke on their yelping.

3

Stillness. Not a sound
in the black world.
The sea of centuries
in death and boredom.

Forests weep
in age-old wilderness.
The blade of a tear
turned eyelashes crimson.

A STONE

1
A stone has no windows,
it has no eyes.
Its silence flows
through our bloodless age.

It's more estranged than the moon,
closer than the space in dreams.
It mutely questions us
via the passionless pulp of sounds.

Thousands of sorrows and joys
beat on the stone in vain –
it will give the gift of its inside
only to tench and deer.

2
At times there is shame with a stone:
the lesson of being aches.
At times we dream about the cathedral
of it that's a century or an instant.

Song takes wing into the cupola
of the depths, wafting to perceived vaults –
then it's no more. It mutes,
into clay, into ashes, into dust.

DON JUAN

Your frivolous age is in Aprils.
Or is it Januaries? In bloom? Or beneath the snow?
The life-driving branches of veins
carry insatiable zeal.

You neither call nor pray. You strike.
Icy pursuit is in your eyes.
In a dummy's embroidered silk lace
your time falls into a stupor, withered.

Like an ancient pagan offering,
like the mark of stalagmite centuries,
the chrysolite of pupils bids
white beasts to fall.

Have you forgotten how a quiet touch
demanded May rights,
how you spun a moonbeam
from the braid of darkness?

The warm-bodied rivers of songs
were quaffed by maidens' lips;
and forever from the embraces of arms
the azure edifice has been growing…

From whom are you running?
Who is he, that mute, stony enemy?
What kind of flaming flood
stains and intoxicates you?

It scourges, rips, contorts, torments
like the lightning bolts of trestles –
and you no longer are an apprentice of May,
but a hired hand of October spasms.

This reeling pursuit
will overcome the boundlessness of sorrows:
an infertile faceless woman
will lie down with you in the sack.

MOZART

The lithe structure of the universe is cast
in fragile snowflakes, in the bursting arrows of leaf veins,
in the prisms of small pieces of glass, in the tension of scales
and in the shadow of a linden on stone slabs.

Rings pulsate across a lake, breath-like,
and with a faithful rhythm the surf smooths sand gravel.
A sudden wind has rushed in from hotter climes,
casting embellishments of spells on bright waters .

A stream like the arc in a restrained blowout
traces the singing bow of the heavens,
and sounds mirror themselves,
like narcissuses in a shimmering stretch of water.

These are not a bird's unconscious warbles
and not a clarinet of forests or horn of storms –
this is the soul of music for and by itself
guiding crystal parallels.

There are no murky anxieties in this music,
just – jokingly – the bitter taste of the unknown.
Go to sleep peacefully: God measured the stars,
and the world swirls in precise axioms.

CHOPIN

1. PRELUDE OF A SPRING EVENING

You are – an intently gray and black
enchanter of ladies' hands.
The scent gives off the air of bedrooms,
and behind windows is the evening myth,
the geometry of promenades.

Maestro! They're asking you to play!
Let the sound-bladed knife tickle the nerves
more tenderly, not to tears.
They love beasts behind bars,
so leave your pain for later.

You'll finish. One more that you
conquered will come to you wistfully:
"Where is your kin? From which roads have you come?
Your play is of burning, boundlessly,
from which there are an angel, fire and sin."

In a garden, in bud-covered silence,
float, fly – and forget for a moment
with intertwining bodies, with an easy lift-off of fusion
that captured by the rigging of sounds,
only the human heart aches this way.

2. ETUDE OF A RAINY MORNING

The wind pierced the stretched silk
of a gossamer morning.
The barefoot rain started along the cobblestones,
like a beggar it knocked on the window glass.

Your lips are whitewashed by chalk,
through your temples – the hum of ailing blood.
With a staff of a cough into the gate of the chest
the ambassador bluntly has pounded.

A monstrous felling in the basalts of halls
with a meat-devouring color of eyes
in the evening again, from under your hands,
will tear the victim's nerves.

The wind rattles the window. A wedge
of thunder. The cough has nagged to death.
Now is – the time. A rotten key –
a bone that's suddenly winged.

In the chest it's larger than that, anxiety:
you – a momentary God – create
over the din, breaking-in, over the enemy's mockery
a small victory of tremolos.

A SMALL POET

I knew him, and it was painful for me.
He spoke of stars, tuberose flowers;
the sweat of tuberculosis covered his hair,[9]
and dark blue lines crossed his brow.

He said that the moon is – a magical tinsmith,
a maker of coins, a golden-browed Buddhist;
that monuments are – just fragile adornments,
and myths of war – small card tables.

In his room, dark and cramped,
he wove words, lean and lisping.
It seemed as if – his finger were striking a bony key,
but failed to meet the strings where songs grew.

It seemed that when he leaves us,
he'll leave us just letters and commas.
But a quiet garden grew in imaginary dreams
to become a world in a slender tome.

---

[9] Mariana Rubchak in an email (dated 9/21/2019) has indicated to me that this poem may be about Bohdan Rubchak's close friend and poet from the New York Group Bohdan Boychuk, who suffered from tuberculosis at the time Rubchak wrote the poem.

MY ITHACA[10]

Sparks of temples are turning ash cool,
pupils are fading along with a song.
Clouds will dream out the gentleness
of your palms from the sky blue of memory.

It's not easy to sail with the baggage of days:
I jettisoned all of this into the sea.
But the reflection of your words keeps
a heart tossed into the sea safe.

I was leaving behind many desires and many homes –
manacle-paths ensnared the body.
I wanted a squall to roar in a word,
so that the word would burn like the wind.

How long I swam, and rowed, and roamed,
a high wind served as a coffin.
I forgot about the peace of shadowy eyebrows,
the calm of windless words.

Now the free will of sailing is – captivity,
and a gloomy, wormwood path.
And I sail into your warmth
like a boat into a white harbor.

---

[10] The home of Odysseus from Homer's *Odyssey*. The poem appears in the second reissue of the original *A Personal Clio* (p. 22) under the title "Odysseus."

A WINTRY ROMANCE

In a tender battle with snow
wind wafts in softly and nimbly,
as though a young lad is welcoming[11]
his lass at a sky-blue station.

The city is – a faraway planet. Just haze.
Ridges, craters, and crags.
A street like a silver arrow
darts to our rendezvous.

Years will pass, words will become frozen,
snow flowers will melt.
Just the memory of You will remain
the tiny world of eternal January.

There will be sun, and tea, and snow –
we'll leave everything the way we found it.
Only a touch of momentary dreams
will become Your lips.

---

[11] In the original published version the lad is saying farewell to his lass.

A SONG FOR MARIANA

This love is like precious fruit,
Mature, late in season.
It's like night that quivers in its
final, autumn song.

I carried this love out of September
for its delicate birdlike nature,
and for eyes that in a blue whisper
beseech beginning.

For hair that pours onto breasts
like torrents of nets,
for palms that in lunar reaches
cast the light of saintliness.

I live in this love as though in
an old, misty garden,
and gather silver beads of joy
in a shady leaf.

I became lost in my love's face
as if I were in a bewildering land:
In its mysterious landscape
I am seeking myself.

1967

NOTES FROM A DIARY

1. THE FIRST POEM

Cigarette butts, streaks of smoke,
portraits of erased words, ghosts
of thoughts, matthiolas shriveled.

And the window, like a longing eye:
beyond it tigers, deer, green lions, horses lie –
clouds in a children's menagerie.

Eyes will nuzzle the poplar tree,
and cheeks will caress white
breasts of winds – above the papers.

Here's the first of nocturnal deviations:
like a morning beam
                      in a cave of autumn forests –
pain shines through a line.[12]

2. OUTSIDE THE WINDOW

Trees languish, weary,
cursed in a flood of gazes,
by the wall of a dead city.

The cruel stone of thought
dishonors a youth of verdure,
maiming the leaves of Aprils.

But the eternal tentacles of roots
meander at primordial midnight
from rootless, bark-less days.

---

[12] This line can also be read as: "a line shines through pain."

Beneath the scabs of pavement,
beneath homeless footsteps they search for
the promised land of a pine wood.

3. A JUSTIFICATION

All the same I am like
a thin little March boy[13]
from those very personal springs,
from the ones – do you remember them?

Somewhere in another world,
They grow like pristine mint.

A memory of them carried by the wind
touches my hot hands,
and in its surges the reason
for my midnight celebrations,

for my strained noondays,
for my mysterious meanings.

In sleepy reaches of memory
odd children's faces,
reflected like ruffled circles –
I catch them in a word's net.

Do you really hear their shrouded weeping
in my myth?

---

[13] Rubchak was born on March 6, 1935.

4. SEVERAL OBSERVATIONS

*

Black poplars weave
the evening expanse
on the looms of branches.

*

The body of a beauty
under lustful fingers:
the moon and a river.

*

In cast nets of a downpour
something silvery flutters:
a lantern fish.

*

A slender brush
paints worlds on glass:
a poplar and the horizon.

*

Spring birds
will awaken groves of pupils:
first love.

*

August fingers
play on molded violins:
that's how pears ripen

*

The white bird of silence is
in the cage of a song.
It is a gift for a lover.

*

Green thoughts
Killed by the frost of words:
the old age of a poet.

DESTINATION[14]

Defiance is fruitless here –
the world won't tell you: "Come back!"
Away from tomorrow and yesterday
the boat will be driven high up.

Farewells will burn, sun,
the circle of infinity:
the banner of your endurance
will be your only friend.

There will be no hugs of home,
nowhere to come to.
You'll feel deadly exhaustion,
but you won't make landing.

---

[14] This poem appears under the rubric of *A Personal Clio* in *The Wing of Icarus*, but does not appear in the original edition.

FROM THE COLLECTION
DROWNING MARENA[15] *(1983)*

....

[15] *Drowning Marena* appeared as part of this first edition of *The Wing of Icarus* in 1983.

DROWNING MARENA[16]

In the opened mouth of a cave
that exhales the parchedness of time,
where, perhaps, spells were muttered,
darkly illuminated by a conjecture,
where feline armor bearers of the night
(with malicious consent from the moon)
piled up skins from bats
and a serpent's silver rings –

in the stone womb of the cave
a rose-colored pearl swelled.

Setting a rumor off on a trail,
cheerful archers searched for what was furthest
in the future from the beginning:
they tormented with whips made of rays,
tying up into a net of the dawn
the goat strawmen of ancestors.
Like a stamp of shame,
red blotches from slaps on the face tingled.

But onlookers didn't veer into the world,
didn't betray the blood flower.

---

[16] The ancient Slavic goddess of night, death, and eternal life, who is associated with winter and whiteness. She is also known as Morana, Morena, and Mara. She is the daughter of the goddess Lada and Lada's husband Svarog. She is known as Mare in Norse mythology. "Mara" (specter) is also part of the root of the word "koshmar" (nightmare) in Ukrainian and possibly "mor" (pestilence). She is the bringer of life and death and often comes in dreams. She asphyxiates people by sitting on their chest in sleep. Straw effigies of Marena dressed in beautiful clothes and adornments would be burned in rituals to bring on the end to winter. She also would be drowned after being burned in effigy to chase away troubles in medieval times. See the following for a brief description in English: http://www.encyclopediaofukraine.com/display.asp?linkpath=pages%5CM%5CA%5CMarena.htm. And note this article in Russian for more details: http://bogislavyan.ru/mara-marena-boginya-smerti/.

She grew, watered by the word,
fed by a warm touch,
emulating the swelling of plums
with their midnight color.
She accepted the sleepy torrents
of her dark Mother,
she gave in to the tightly caressing
mouths of liana vines –

far from the noisy ranks,
the descending of insatiable huntsmen.

In the opened mouth of a cave
the goddess parted with her Mother
to enter our nightmares
as an eager bride,
to stir up myriad feuds
above the black expanse of demise,
to grow as the queen of mirages,
calling herself Marena.

but trappers fettered the captive,
drowned her in the lake of morning.

LETTER TO HOME

I'm fed up, you know, of reaping rye in December
and of being on the lookout for grapes in January,
of dragging on again a colossal parable
back into eternity like a knight on stage.

Like mirages that stand guard over a word–
are your touches. Like an escort to a nightmare.
Like those poplars, Gothic by memories,
that you can't live through by flying over.

So what are we to do? We who exist
neither in my nor in your future?
Will we really forever poison with a mugwort potion
my stretched-tight blood, my bloody weekdays?

We'll turn into stone in the delusive distance
like old indiscernible statues.

A BOOK FROM HOME

Well, really, shoo, hey there, Mykyta:[17]
a stranger will tell us about everything in the world.
Muscovite envy and Tatar anger
are hidden in his crocodile eyes.

He survives by dazzling deftness,
for he thinks guiltily and eats guiltlessly:
he tied up a belowground evil spirit
or aboveground tidings like periwinkle to a trough.

May he not strum for us to show he's a blessed simpleton,
the son of a sweet land and salt of the sweet earth:
pedantically in a surgeon's glove,
to cut open a Poet's pupils –
here the shrewd stranger is a master by all odds.

The apprentice of evil. The bastard of the Antichrist.

---

[17] Rubchak seems to have in mind here Kyrylo Kozhumiaka and his son Mykyta, whose surname means "tanner," or literally "one who makes leather soft." Mykyta is a *bohatyr*, one of the mighty heroes of Ukrainian folklore. In the folktales about him, he agrees to fight a dragon to save a princess after twelve orphan children, the third group of inhabitants of Kyiv to make the request of him, bring him to tears with their plea. After defeating the dragon in battle, Mykyta asks for nothing in return for his good deed, and the Prince as a reward names the spot where Mykyta lives in Kyiv "Kozhumiake" (Tanner's Place).

DECADENCE

1.

Autumn, like an agile coquette
from distant days,
that in the worn portrait of an ancestor,
at the bottom of a goblet

sees fiery eyes, rotted through,
and feels pity,
and in a stiffened body sways
its first waltz.

2.

Like a frail nobleman
in a dirty bistro,
autumn raises a toast
to dead chambers, to posh beds;

something noticeable is in the fragile movements,
like the sediment of holidays,
and, like gloom, its long-live toast shuffles
along the cobblestones.

A FLASH AND A REFLECTION

An aspen grove in January
in the crumpled strings of death
echoless sounds grew numb
last year's maimed leaves.

The white-crusted stream will not
hear them, for it is mute today
in benumbed restraint –
it won't repeat them fluidly,

to it for the green holidays,
won't wash the blue scarves.
From both of them frightened little animals
will not drink their fill of words.

The specter of a branchy elk
in an ossified trot
will fade away in a misty mirror
like a two-part voice of prematurity.

A MANDARIN FOR MY WIFE

When, having outshined myself,
like a god, saturated with perpetuity,
covered in a stone smile,
I will step onto the edge, the first and last;

when in the morning millions of stares
will wrap the solitary me into a shroud,
and in a golden arc will harden
all my yearnings and indecisions –

curb your crying, and under sweet cherry leaves
start off alone that roadside day.

A baby beggar, smeared all over,
is playing there in the mud. His gaze is
open and empty, and a breeze has begun to waft
in a soft circular flow onto his hair.

THE FEMALE SAINT AND THE DEVIL[18]

In the cocoons of icons windows grew numb,
and sleepy thighs are in the broadcloth of all-night vigil keepers.
Multicolored moments of April
ripen in the gold of age-old mosaics.

Hands fell on a faceless maple tree,
instead of sleeping in the interlacing of veiny arms,
living in curly-sloped beddings,
and laying my caresses on the twins.

You're a chambermaid of words and a reaper of mirages.
As though in niches, turned chaff-like yellow,
in your motionless eyes
the wings of doves have turned to stone.

I'd maim your lips with splinters of laughter,
I'd adorn your cheeks with ripples of dolor –
for your face's tranquil day
is like the dreadful void of God.

---

[18] Rubchak may have in mind the image/icon of St. Marina of Antioch, who lived in the third century and was known as a demon-slayer. For information on her see the following description of her at the website of a Coptic parish named after her: https://stmarina.org/our-church/life-of-saint-marina-of-antioch/.

SKETCHES

1. A MADRIGAL

Teensily bro
ken is my lady.[19]

The beads of her eyes
quiver in mine. The allure
of lips on me.
Trembling.

A snow of touches drift
ed onto dreams –
thinking about the twins
of my lover's body,
so that every cell of my brain

is bathed in its honey.

In the prism of vision
her shine is shat
tered. In the mélange of night
a dimly lit swarm
of tiny planets:

her brow – a monastery
her thighs –
a Turkish paradise,

---

[19] An alternate reading of these lines could be: "Teensily the skirt/my lady allure."

her hair – the rain
her palms – the snow,
her lips turn into a – smile,
but her eyes somehow are in tears.

So strangely bro
ken is my lady.[20]

2. COMPLAINING ABOUT DECEMBER

Laboriously the year dies
like an old believer.

Laboriously cold-handed
December
gives me back my memories
of the state
of your eyes,
eyebrows,
and breasts.

It's an old miser!

It entices
with your face
in the sinews of branches.

---

[20] An alternate reading of these lines could be: "So wondrously the skirt/ my lady allure."

THE GODS[21]
(From W.S. Merwin)

Once they thronged on the threshold of mortality
But were not chosen
There is no such freedom as theirs
For those who have no beginning

Even the wind is their memory
Estates where they cannot live
And in which they never are absent

What are you, they ask, *you simply exist*,
And the heavens and earth bow to them
Raising a glance from above their choices
Dying

All day all night
Everything that is mistaken adores them
Even the dead sing an infinite anthem to them.

---

[21] American "academic" poet W.S. Merwin (1927-2019) and contemporary of Rubchak who often refers to the literature of antiquity as well as other literary works in his poetry similarly to Rubchak. Rubchak is probably referring here to two of Merwin's poems: "The Gods" and "To the Gods." Merwin's meditations on mortality would have also attracted the poet.

FROM THE COLLECTION
THE WING OF ICARUS (1983; 1991)

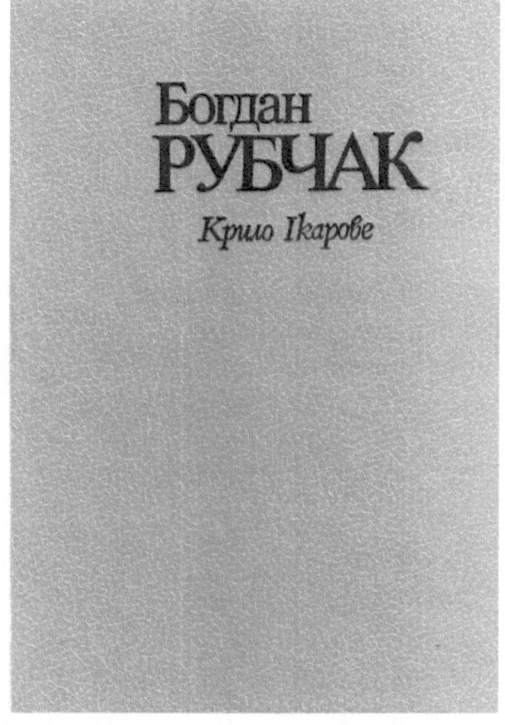

THE BLACKSMITH

Heavenly blacksmiths forge songs
that render the blue body of the world;
on the muscle of the heart iron kings
chisel a mark of lightning for us.

The blacksmith was forging in a grimy village
of some dismal district.
On the bench of a *gazda* – are word-tellers of a myth
of a bright burning raging earth.

He pulls out golden embryos
from his hearth. In stern self-oblivion
he teaches them to sing in protoforms.

And something small snuggles in the corner,
it's so red-haired, big-eyed, and shaggy –
it's learning how to forge its own songs.

RAIN

You unfolded into infinite drops.
The ticking of moments for you – is syncopated.
You stroke the faces of others like yourself,
because your flow won't smooth out your own.

I envy you, from a multitude – one.
In dry minutes my lengthy time expires.
Though your lustful touch on my face will dash by –
it won't smooth out granite specks of dust.

A sculpture, new in its incessantness,
from these wonderfully self-wasting-away meshworks –
what an artist of amusing allurements and boldness!

I wish I could find the courage to disregard
my dismal impediments: to fall on the wet earth
in generously unsigned words.

AN EVENING PRAYER

Take me across the night in your boat,
tipsy old man. The shore will be waiting
for morning with the drought of craving
and with the flood of my love's tear.

Don't prattle about some sweet islands
in hundred-voiced thickets of dozing off,
and don't entice me with the rage of burning out,
or threaten me with a midnight squall.

I'll give you these several words for your
ungodly labor. You'll thank me insincerely
and bury them in the dirt of rags.

After sailing away under a goatskin sail
back into the night, you'll pass judgment over them
and set them loose to dance with the black whirlpool.

1983

NARCISSUS

He pleads before the mirror: "Forgive me!"
And again he goes – headlong to the book stacks:
like in catacombs, sample skulls,
there lie dreams, diaries, and letters.

He takes to wandering through someone
else's life, pecking at submissive pages,
picking out choice words from them –
to save his life with an archetype.

And when deceitful images grow loathsome,
again he combs the storage rooms
in his very own masks – to carry them again
to new cities and to unfamiliar bridges.

And again he enters into an insatiable mirror,
To plead for forgiveness from it again.

THE HARDEST GAME

I'm a true doyen of peculiar relations –
of odious abbey conspiracies in silver mountains,
and of the words that you uttered yesterday
while you were putting dishes on a shelf.

A double-meaning look, fiery but restrained,
your gait, rambling and swift,
they suggested certain lines from Tagore
and nimble dances of wind dervishes.

What metaphors these are! It's time for me
to release them in the wind along with Tagore,
because I'm no master of these games, but a slave.

The most difficult game before me is this:
whether to cherish or trample flowers –
to understand you in your entirety.

DRAMATURGY

I've lived through our lifegiving sin,
that game of ours, an April and autumn one.
But you keep coming and going just like a shadow,
just like the figures in my dreams.

I already have a new "Theater of Diversions"
in an old building that chases away decay;
but sometimes I pray to that stone
from which your laughter has been made.

For others you'll be a sorrowful mask,
a small role – or their destiny,
deeming their every fall and failure.

For me you'll become neither a swallow
nor an owl, but will remain yourself –
the same way I created you.

COMPRESSIONS

* * *

Once my time used to waft onto me like a brother,
like spring that used to cozy up to me –
to reveal everything in me that's speechless,
green, my swaddled secrets.

Now my time caws at me like a raven,
it roars with laughter in swirling fallen leaves,
and drags my letters along umber cobblestones
so that deceitful eyes of stars would read them.

* * *

This apple tree was like a sister to me,
in spring it was resurrected into a white gleam
and fed me with earthly joy,
watered my suffering with nourishment.

When I was with it at the time of blossoming
as the white annunciation of the Holy Mother –
a hobo came from an unknown light
to cut us apart with the blatant barb of a word.

* * *

Muffled uneasiness in leaves and flowers
disquiets my hearing and keeps me from reading.
Is this for the rain? I come to the window
to ask the cherry tree about the weather.

Onto the folio of a flower bed, where words
are like a wreath, the sky gives vague citations.

I and the small cherry tree outside the window
read them. We fear the reading ending.

* * *

In the intensity of boundless years
countless machines work together –
to compose its own myth about the green world,
to typeset a story of returning.

They will cut you down, tie you into rafts,
lumberman hastily will toss you onto saws.

On the white scraps of souls in dark gray seams
someone else's bloody matters will be typeset
by insatiable bustling ants.

* * *

I've fashioned a cage of words for you
to lock you in like a finch.
I've woven a translucent net of hints
to capture and forget you.

When I playfully fed you
with crumbs of conjectures from my palm,
how could I have known that my words
have already been serving in your captivity for a while?

* * *

Again he is strange. Tufts of thoughts and smoke.
With a pen he chases something on paper.
She both loves him and doesn't,
she knows him and doesn't.

Is he a god or lichen? A river or underriver?
The slave of winged-equine spirits or web-footed ones?
This night he will not be her man again,
he must send her a swan.

* * *

A great chunk of the sun broke off
when you were born. Look!
From it, you, when the day was dying down,
used to light up all over with laughter.

Look. Your planet is floating away
into that space that has already given me shelter.
Like the star in the song of an ancient poet,
it either grows pale or fades in the distance.

Bohdan and Mariana Rubchak
celebrating Mariana's birthday in Kyiv, 1993

AFTERWORD I
MY LIFE WITH THE POET AND HIS POETRY

MARIAN J. RUBCHAK

Bohdan Rubchak's ashes – deposited in his personal *Stone Garden*

In 1956 twenty-one-year-old Bohdan Rubchak published his first collection of poetry, in Ukrainian – *The Stone Garden (Kaminnyi sad)*. It begins with the poem "In a Room of a Hundred Mirrors," revealing considerable introspection and a rare self-understanding in one so young (written in October 1955). I begin with this poem with the expectation that it will provide a useful aid to a more profound appreciation of Bohdan as a person, a poet, and a man who spent most of his adult life concealing an essential part of himself – his inner life – behind masks and games. Svitlana Budzhak-Jones, co-translator of this volume, describes his poetry as follows: ". . . when one considers his innovative use of words, integrating borrowings from other languages, and the convoluted syntax, it becomes a puzzle, a riddle, a task, and a game, all in one." Her analysis explains the difficulties (impossibility), with some rare exceptions, of unpacking one of Bohdan's poems. In the absence of the essential qualifications for a professional literary analysis, and in the interest of a more nuanced perception of his work, I have chosen to offer some personal observations on the circumstances under which Bohdan wrote some of his poems. I focus primarily, although not exclusively, on the ones that I am able to make some sense of because they relate to me in one way or another. Before I move on to further comments, here is a stanza from that revealing first poem:

> In a room of a hundred mirrors, I, self-loving,
> see myself beautifully distorted. And only
> in the gray garden of stone walls – on their surface –
> my reflection can never betray me.

Bohdan was a multi-talented poet and scholar with a finely-honed intellect, cultivated by his passion for knowledge and incessant reading. Admittedly, this passion did take time from his own writing, something he acknowledged, even obsessively dwelled upon, but never managed to change: it also enriched his poetry. A more compelling impediment to his talent and productivity harkened back to 1947 when Bohdan lost a significant role model – his father – who died in Germany after time spent in a post-war DP camp. Bohdan was a sensitive twelve-year-old at the time, still in the formative stage of development who, following that painful loss; became exceedingly dependent on his scheming mother. After losing a husband at a relatively young age, she was determined to hold on to her son as a surrogate. To ensure this she raised him as an immature dependent child and took control of his life by performing tasks for which he should have been responsible. The most visible manifestation of her influence was his wardrobe. His mother determined what he wore and insisted on making the selections for him, with the result that he was dressed in the conventional image of his late father. When he began earning money in his early teens, she took charge of his finances, so that he never learned to handle or value money. There was a fine irony in this because Bohdan was the son of the president of a financial institution in his native Ukraine. His financial ineptitude led to disastrous lifelong consequences, marked by Bohdan's failure to control his reckless spending. He incessantly lamented his debts yet continued to pile on new ones even before the old ones had been cleared, then bemoaned the fact that no one was willing to help him. I helped him substantially, but it was never enough because he continued to incur new debts. More importantly, the consequences of those sixteen early years of training severely impacted his literary output, his self-confidence, and his self-esteem. This unfortunate development became impressed on his work, creating numerous writing blocks. Bohdan told me on several occasions that he was also constantly reminded by his mother to cultivate modesty, to avoid seeking fame and glory. Instead of chasing public esteem he should find a nice quiet corner and write for his own pleasure. Bohdan internalized that advice; it eroded the breadth of his writing, along with his productivity. Seemingly reluctant to blame the true source, he blamed himself at first: "I ruined my life and my talent. I betrayed myself, and most important, my heart (referring to his devotion to writing)," he wrote in his diary (January 17, 1980). To compound the damage, hanging over Bohdan like an albatross, was his endless anxiety over his mother's ill health, her allegedly failing heart (she outlived him by twelve years.) For decades it served as an effective device for ensuring his compliance with her will.

On the occasion of his dreaded fiftieth birthday Bohdan took stock of his life. He summed it up with new confessions: "Too much reading, too little writing, too much TV! All of this is attributable to my mother, who raised me this way." The following year he wrote in a related entry: "I was never taught to value my time, or my money. She (*mamusia;* her preferred form of address) instilled in me a false sense of time in which to achieve my goals, and as for money somehow it always seemed to appear just when I really needed it or worse, it led me to resort to borrowing from friends. Nor was I encouraged to behave responsibly, to accept any culpability for my actions, and I was never taught to share. I recognize this now, but how to apply such insights to real life? This regrettable upbringing formed my lack of maturity, my childishness. Perhaps [Bohdan] Boychuk was right after all," he went on to muse, "now I habitually wait for 'mother Ukraine' [or some other mother] to 'breastfeed me'" (May 25, 1985). This painful soul searching was rooted in Bohdan's Janus-like existence – the public persona of an engaging, entertaining, witty man, characterized by our friend and colleague Michael Naydan as "a man who was smart, sharp, witty, fun, fascinating" (e-mail, Sept. 21, 2019), but with the dark interior of a severely tortured soul.

1963 became a defining year for Bohdan. It served as a kind of "rite of passage," although later he did complain that even its promise had fallen short of his expectations (March 19, 1984). The catalyst for this major re-examination of himself was his mother's ill-conceived reaction to Bohdan's return, on January 1, 1963 from a vacation in New York City. He had spent a euphoric ten days making the acquaintance of long-admired literati – giants of Ukrainian literature, members of the New York Group of Poets to which he belonged, and participating in stimulating literary events that included enthusiastically received readings of his own poetry. Understandably elated by this New York experience, he returned home in a state of euphoria, together with a determined resolve to build on his newly awakened pride in himself, to begin writing with renewed purpose, unaware that *mamusia* was already busy perfecting her skills for the performance of her life. For its enactment, worthy of an award-winning histrionic presentation, she drew on her well-tried arsenal of castigations, used in the past with such astonishing success. Upon Bohdan's homecoming she unleashed an impressive range of accusations, invectives, orders, warnings, reproaches, admonitions, and directives on a dutiful son's appropriate behavior and concern for his ailing mother.

Although *mamusia's* performance had risen to the level of a consummate actress, unknown to her it had lost its edge. She had let the magical genie out of the bottle and that artful creature refused to let it back in. Bohdan referred to this unfortunate diatribe in his diary but never revealed his reaction to it, although early traces of changes in him soon began to come to light.

Meanwhile, he returned to his former relationship with Francesca, (January 3, 1963 diary entry – hereafter only dates). Bohdan described his first post-NYC encounter with her, as tender, yet paradoxically the following day he described that meeting as a failed exercise in reaching some kind of accommodation with her. He also resumed active contact with his Chicago friends but now, for the first time, described their conversations as empty and banal. Bohdan's New York experience had clearly changed him. Although he performed brilliantly in school (I met his professors who attested to this) he started showing signs of losing interest in his studies, and soon abandoned them. Shortly afterward he was awarded a master's equivalent degree from the University of Chicago in recognition of his brilliant performance in class.

Several months later he wrote in his diary about another concern: "I have become disgusted with my masks. I have played enough games in my life to make me forget who I am, to wonder what I have been protecting in myself. At the same time I find it so difficult to ignore my person" (July 8, 1963). Bohdan recognized this as an attempted escape from himself, from his immaturity, and addressed it in his autobiographical poem "Don Juan," published in *A Personal Clio* (1967), but that was the extent of his effort to change anything:

> From whom are you running?
> Who is he, that mute, stony enemy?
> What kind of flaming flood
> stains and intoxicates you?

With a more normal upbringing, a less traumatic early life filled with loss, and the shock of his wartime experience he might have avoided some of those demons that were lining up to torment him even further. In describing his situation he asserted: "Things would be so much easier if I was able to reach some sort of reconciliation with myself. I am too focused on myself, and this rules out inner peace" (January 16, 1963). "I am constantly with myself." Then came an important admission: "At some crucial moment in my childhood I lacked the strength to stand up for myself, to defend myself" (January 30, 1963). In a January 30 diary entry he added: "I live as if in a fog, as though I am not really my own self. I have even lost the desire to break out of this lethargy."

On May 5 of that year he made a diary entry with some advice to himself: "I must stop wasting time with people who have little to offer me. What I need is a better understanding of myself and my potential. Living on the edge [of life] is of no use, so is squandering my life on meaningless trivialities. At the same time it is very difficult to forget myself."

Before the month of July was over Bohdan recognized that fate had already taken a hand in his effort to find himself. Somewhat earlier he had received an offer to join the faculty at the University of Manitoba, in its Slavic Department. He first wrote about it in his diary on July 31 but did not come to any decision at that time After some vacillation and considerable soul searching, he decided to "bite the bullet," to ignore his trepidation over leaving the nest and standing on his own two feet, making independent decisions. Once before Bohdan had attempted to establish his independence by enlisting for a tour of duty in Korea in 1958 in order to "get away from my mother," he once explained to me, only to discover how much he loved and missed her (which he did not explain). I learned about their close ties from his voluminous correspondence that I read after his death. His letters were filled with endearing terms, some of them rather embarrassing for a 23-year-old man writing to his mother. *Mamusia's* skill in keeping him tied to her was never more in evidence. Her ability to exert her will extended beyond that as well. This tiny four foot ten-inch woman took on the most powerful military machine in the world, the United States Army, and secured Bohdan's early discharge after he had served ten months. One can only view with awe such amazing resourcefulness.

Following his tour of duty in Korea, Bohdan fell deeply in love (irrevocably he believed) with an American heiress to a considerable oil fortune whom he named Francesca, although her real name was Larisa. I have no idea when or where they met, but from what Bohdan told me about a serious involvement with a Ukrainian girl while he was in Japan during his Korean service, it appears unlikely that Francesca and he could have been involved, or perhaps been acquainted, before the end of 1958. Although he had believed it to be a permanent relationship, at the close of 1959 Bohdan walked away from this romantic attachment. Poems published in the collection *The Radiant Betrayal* (1960) point to the intense pain he experienced over this breakup, but he did not reconsider. In a conversation early in our marriage, Bohdan talked about suffering over a heartbreaking deception, and his retaliation: "I went right out and betrayed her." Was a betrayal the cause of his break with Francesca? It seems likely, but why tell me about it? Was it meant as a cautionary tale? His first poetic reference to the break is a poem titled "The Radiant Betrayal," published in his third collection under the same title. In that poem he also ponders his own guilt in contributing to this infidelity:

> You need more solitude
> than the one in four walls:
> you need to fall on your knees
> inside of yourself forever.

Bohdan and Francesca were destined to meet again, in New York this time, in late December of 1962. He described their encounter as "superficial, empty," yet seemed to regret his own insincere behavior. "It appears that I might have walked away from our affair too soon," he mused (January 1, 1963). Shortly afterward he reflected on it: "I was thinking about Francesca – perhaps. . ." (January 2, 1963), but I never found another reference to a meeting with her, until they ran into each other in Chicago at some time in the eighties. He came home in a high state of agitation and told me about it.

Excerpts from two additional poems about Francesca suggest lingering vestiges of distress. In the poem "For Francesca" he wrote:

> Why are you here, why? Your worlds have wilted
> beyond the point measured by Mondays. To whom
> are you bringing offerings by the thousands
> voiceless, pointed ones – every night?

And "For Francesca Again," (The original version, titled "For Someone Close," on pp. 132 -133 in *Krylo Ikarove*):

> You conceal the apocalypse beneath your
> eyelids. In my rib cage an unforgivable beast
> is quieting down. An assemblage of pointy-blue stars
> wants to burn out what's left of my brain.
>
> The adorned hand of the mighty world will
> tear up even our recollection of an image and
> something infinitely tender, something
> living will wither, without waiting for a response.

After the breakup Bohdan spent roughly two years in an affectionate relationship with Oksana, a woman from his close circle of Chicago friends. He now sought a less dramatic, less passionate, more serene attachment (January 5, 1963). The charming, witty Oksana, with her sparkling personality, appeared to be a good choice. As the relationship deepened, however, it evolved into an increasingly troubled one. It appears that she was as neurotic, as conflicted as Bohdan himself. Her erratic behavior toward him was apparently the unfortunate result of control by a no less overbearing parent (her father) than Bohdan's mother was. This could account for her pattern of mysterious disappearances and sudden reappearances. Although Bohdan conceded that he did not understand her as much as he would have wished, for him she still represented a "good solution to his loneliness" (January 3, 1963). Solution to his loneliness? But, curiously, no mention of love....

During one of Oksana's prolonged absences, Bohdan indulged in one amorous adventure after another, but found something lacking in each one. In a diary entry dated January 5, 1963 he suggested his own culpability in the failure of these liaisons, explaining that he lacked the strength (motivation?) to commit himself to one woman, to love her truly, to "make her his own" (January 4, 1963). After yet another extended absence Oksana reappeared as suddenly as she had disappeared, only this time Bohdan responded with: "She keeps calling and calling, Why? Our affair isn't going anywhere" (April 26, 1963). And yet he remained unwilling to abandon the relationship altogether in the faint hope that their problems might somehow resolve themselves. A series of poems related to their affair were published in *To The Girl without a Country* (1963): "A Sleepless Night;" "The Dancer;" "The Destination;" and "The Farness of Roads."

* * *

How did I come into Bohdan's life? I too had arrived at a life-changing decision back in 1961. At the age of thirty I decided to resume my education, interrupted by raising a family. By 1963, at the age of thirty-two, some careful planning enabled me to become a full-time degree student at the University of Manitoba. On September 18, 1963 I proceeded to my initial class meeting. A wolf-whistle nearby attracted my attention for a moment. I learned later that it was Bohdan, who asked my friend Robert Klymash, an instructor in the same Slavic Department: "Who is that lovely lady?" to which Klymash responded: "Careful, she is married with four children." At the same time I learned that Bohdan had shrugged this off with: "I don't care."

Taking a front-row seat I joined the class in awaiting the arrival of our new professor. Soon, in walked Bohdan, a charismatic young man exuding charm and magnetism. A serious confusion in classroom assignments on the part of the administration resulted in our early dismissal after we had exhausted five attempts to find a home for our class. We agreed to meet the next day. As I was leaving I happened to glance at my schedule once more and noticed that I had inadvertently enrolled for too many class meetings in a single day. Apparently my concentration skills needed some work if I hoped to function successfully as a degree student. Regretfully, I requested a drop slip. Bohdan's unexpected response? "Come with me to my office. We'll see what can be arranged." He made some quick changes to his timetable, conveniently still in flux, and suddenly my schedule fell into place. Unfortunately, this cost him half his class enrollment, but I remained. Then he invited me to accompany him to lunch, where we were joined by Klymash. Together we enjoyed an hour of cheerful banter. More meetings were destined to follow.

Five days later, on September 23, while sharing a faculty elevator with Bohdan on the way to class, I suddenly felt a compelling surge of magnetic energy, a kind of excitement coursing through my body that caused me to turn toward him. In that unspoken moment we both recognized that something extraordinary had just passed between us. In that moment an exciting new chapter had opened in our lives, one that forever changed us both. Bohdan and I continued to see each other for the remainder of the academic year, into the 1964 summer break. By late summer, after a brief separation, my divorce was finalized, and I became a free agent. Although there were numerous other contenders for Bohdan's affections, all hating me of course, we had already become an inseparable couple, notwithstanding that I was encumbered by four daughters. Bohdan chose to overlook this minor impediment – an act of a very brave man.

One of our favorite outings consisted of visits to our favorite restaurant – The Happy Vineyard – with a strolling accordion player who soon parked himself alongside our table. In no time, we were joined by most of the patrons in the dining room for a protracted sing along. Then, a group of our new-found friends accompanied us to my apartment, where I had a piano; and there were three pianists among us. I soon retired but the singing continued until dawn, and later that morning I stumbled upon sleeping guests strewn throughout the apartment. They had all spent the night there. The restaurant scene, so often repeated in various ways and different venues, reflected Bohdan's irrepressible gift for drawing people to himself.

We spent much of that summer in the company of some colorful adult students from Bohdan's classes. One named Otto described himself as a "floor layer from Vancouver." He fell in love with my classmate Marsha, much to the displeasure of his wife Rita. Marsha gleefully (cynically?) put him through some challenging paces by proposing some activities – this time it was several hours of horseback riding – calculated to call attention to their huge age difference. Poor Otto. He limped back to my apartment after it was all over and asked: "Do you have Band-Aids?" He used my entire pack. The second companion was a Hungarian by the name of Haraszty (I never knew his given name), who trolled for women on campus wearing a cape. When he found one he liked, he threw his cape over his shoulder in what he imagined was a romantic gesture and burst into song – "Cheket Kishla."

Unfortunately for this would-be lover the results were always disappointing. A third companion was named Ron (who wrote poetry to me – as Mrs. Kmetyk – still my surname at the time). This amusing trio, together with Marsha, became our frequent companions throughout that blissful summer.

Toward the end of those carefree vacation days, so full of enchantment and promise, an ominous cloud suddenly cast its dark pall over our relationship. Somehow Bohdan's mother had learned of our plans to marry and immediately rushed to Winnipeg bent on damage control. Emphasizing her ailing heart she convinced Bohdan to resign his position at the university and return to Chicago. Fearing for her health, Bohdan acquiesced and soon followed his mother in the hope of calming her fears and sparing a heart attack. She calculated that when he rejoined his old friends in familiar Chicago surroundings he would soon forget me. During the next few problem-filled months she engaged in some desperate schemes to change his mind, to help him forget me, with little success. He was faring no better in his efforts to pacify her. We communicated almost daily by mail and telephone; the calls made to the rhythm of her vacuum cleaner each time he picked up the receiver.

During Bohdan's absence I worked to support myself and my four daughters on very little money, wondering what the future held for us. Their birth father was not offering any assistance, even when one of the girls fell ill. My friend Dorothy Bilash was my greatest support. When my daughter Tania fell ill with a communicable disease Dorothy took her into her home despite having her own toddler in the house. These were dismal months for both Bohdan and me, but our memories and our hopes sustained us until that magical month of January, a month that figures so prominently in Bohdan's poetry.

Mamusia's scheming reached its apotheosis in a final, frenetic attempt to neutralize his decision, related to me later in Chicago, by my new friend Zhorzh. *Mamusia* offered him a bribe of $100 "to get rid of me." The method for my removal was not specified but her proposal, as described by Zhorzh with gusto, became a topic of widespread amusement among Bohdan's friends and acquaintances. It did leave me wondering, however: A paltry $100? Was that the offensive value she placed on me?

Calling to mind a poem by Robert Burns, "To a Mouse" (1786), we are prompted to remember that even the best-laid schemes of mice and men can go awry. The two schemes crafted that fall in 1964 did fail. *Mamusia's* elaborate plans went awry; Bohdan did not forget me. For the first time in his life he found the courage to leave her to her fate, and to her promised heart attacks – that naturally never materialized. Miraculously, the ailing heart had withstood the incredible energy expended on hours of standing behind the closed door to Bohdan's room berating him day after day, week after week. He rejoined me in Winnipeg, and we were married on January 22, 1965. January came to signify the poetic symbol of our private little world.

Having eaten very little on our wedding day, Bohdan drank a bit too much, then went outside for a walk. He spied a ten-foot bank of newly fallen soft white snow and in his inebriated state it must have looked like an inviting, fluffy nuptial bed, into which he happily sank. Bohdan's best man, our lawyer Barry, and I extricated him and put him to bed. When he sobered up in the morning, he showed no sign of recalling this or, it seems, much of anything else that had transpired on that unconventional wedding night in the snow. The next day, my dearest and most loyal friend Dorothy Bilash held a small celebratory reception for us to mark the occasion in a more dignified manner. There was no mention of a snowy nuptial bed.

At the end of the month we packed up our possessions, made beds for my daughters in the back of an old, non too reliable station wagon that I had purchased from the proceeds of the sale of a few items, and set off for Chicago. The trip was more eventful than we had anticipated owing to the failure of certain gauges, including a gas gauge that stopped working. In the middle of the night in snowy, bitter cold Minnesota we ran out of gas. We woke up a sympathetic filling station owner, who looked at our predicament and reopened his station to sell us fuel. When we arrived in Chicago many hours later it was raining – something we Canadians had never seen in January. There, an ominous new surprise awaited us.

As mentioned above, before he left for Winnipeg Bohdan had rented an apartment for us. It was in a dangerous neighborhood, and it came with a set of difficult problems, although they proved to be nothing compared to those that awaited us inside the apartment upon our arrival. We were greeted at the door by *mamusia,* who had installed herself, uninvited (she never seemed to need an invitation), in our apartment. She had appropriated the best room in the house, where she set up her TV to keep it out of the hands of the excited children, relegating all four daughters to the tiny remaining bedroom. Still, *mamusia* lost no time in complaining about her unsatisfactory accommodation. This prompted Bohdan, with his customary sense of wry humor, to suggested sharing the living room with·his books. My daughters had already discovered the joys of those books and, much to Bohdan's consternation, used them to play a game that they named "Who can build the highest bridge?" *Mamusia* remained where she was.

As a wedding gift, she presented me with a floor-length flannel nightgown, with sleeves down to my wrists and a neckline up to my chin. Having thus established her legitimacy as a useful member of the family, each evening she parked herself at the entrance to our bedroom and talked us to sleep. Just as well, Bohdan consoled me. With her tin ear she might have tried singing us to sleep. On Valentine's Day Bohdan thoughtfully used his meager resources to bring me a modest box of chocolates. I passed them around and when I got to her she made a typical scene. She pointed out that Bohdan had never marked this special occasion, with its message to sweethearts, to bring her candy. At first I thought that such a remark was inappropriate from a mother, but recently a news item on our local television channel caught my attention. A newscaster informed his viewers that a third of the pet-owning population in America planned to buy treats for their dogs for Valentine's Day. Had I been too hasty in questioning her disappointment? Among other noteworthy scenes, one took place at our dinner table when I attempted to establish some kind tradition in our new family. I asked Bohdan to take his place at the head of the table, a request that instantly propelled his mother to the phone to call a friend and ask: "What are you having for dinner? They refuse to feed me here." As if such scenes were not enough, and apparently unaware that each outgoing call was recorded in our monthly bill, every day she called Bohdan at work to inform him that I was phoning my "husband" in Canada,

Mamusia's antics finally tried even long-suffering Bohdan's patience, and he suggested that she might be happier in her own place. She went, but she did not "go quiet into the night." An interesting example of her insatiable need for control can be illustrated by a bizarre example after her departure. *Mamusia* adopted a small dog for companionship. After some three weeks in her care the hapless animal succumbed to a "nervous breakdown" (stress anxiety in dogs). It was soon removed, and *mamusia* abandoned further plans for companionship, choosing instead to focus her energy on Bohdan's choice of a wife once more.

Because we were unable to make ends meet on Bohdan's salary I quickly found a position in an advertising agency. As I prepared for my first day of work, *mamusia* innocently inquired: "What about the little one. What are you going to do with her?" She had promised to look after Stasia but went back on her word. I called the agency and Judy, a sympathetic personnel officer offered to hold the job for a month. During this time I was able to install Stasia in a nursery school and was free to take up my new position.

A few weeks later our windows were shot out, and we were robbed. This second occurrence had a ridiculous sequel. While working in a small garden in front of her building our fat old landlady spied the thief carrying off some of our possessions, as she informed us later. Instead of calling the police she hurriedly tried to cover her legs lest he attempt to take a peek at them. We soon moved to an apartment in a marginally better neighborhood that came with its own set of troubles. For one, the owner's "grampa," with time on his hands, spent some of it in periodic house cleaning, throwing out what he considered junk. My entire collection of hats and the children's winter boots were relegated to the junk pile. I never wore hats again; the children outgrew their boots; and we survived two more years of this and other foolishness.

In 1966 Bohdan lost his position at La Salle Extension University after missing 95 days of work according to the administration. He spent a year at home writing prose in English, a new genre for him. Before writing a line he opened a bank account in his name alone because he had decided to become a prominent American novelist who would earn a great deal of money. He had no time to realize his dream because our plans changed once more stemming from a new offer. It was likely during this time that he wrote much of his fourth poetry collection *A Personal Clio*, dedicated to me, although I was not aware of either the collection or the dedication until after his passing.

Meanwhile, he continued to seek inner peace, to recover his lost selfhood. As always, he looked for it in palliatives outside himself instead of facing the fact that the key lay within him. This is expressed in the final stanza of the exquisite "A Song for Mariana," written for me, and judged by many readers to be the most beautiful love poems in the Ukrainian language. For all of its beauty and dedication to me, however, a look at the last line also illustrates a deeply personal need:

> I became lost in my love's face
> as if I were in a bewildering land:
> In its mysterious landscape
> I am seeking myself.

A related poem titled "My Ithaca" was published in the same collection. In the process of translating it, Michael Naydan made a very interesting observation. He suggested a connection to Odysseus' love of and return to Penelope after years of travel and amorous adventures. "I assume you are his Penelope," Michael ventured. Let me paraphrase his full observation: The meaning of Bohdan's turning to Odysseus as a model is the fact that he finds himself associating with the Greek hero. While Odysseus goes out to sea on his great quest and braves the dangers on the sea of life, his true love and his true happiness Penelope was at home, right before his eyes, metaphorically speaking. It took all of his wanderings for him to realize that. "I do think the idea of Penelope for him represents the ideal of true unwavering love" (e mail, November 12, 2019). I could not have said it better. Was it a metaphor for his tortuous journey in quest of his lost selfhood? Was it an acknowledgement of having found a direction toward his hoped-for true home, of some expectation of making peace with himself?

I discovered a fascinating drawing by Bohdan that creates a visual symbol of this Odysseus-like search for Ithaca.

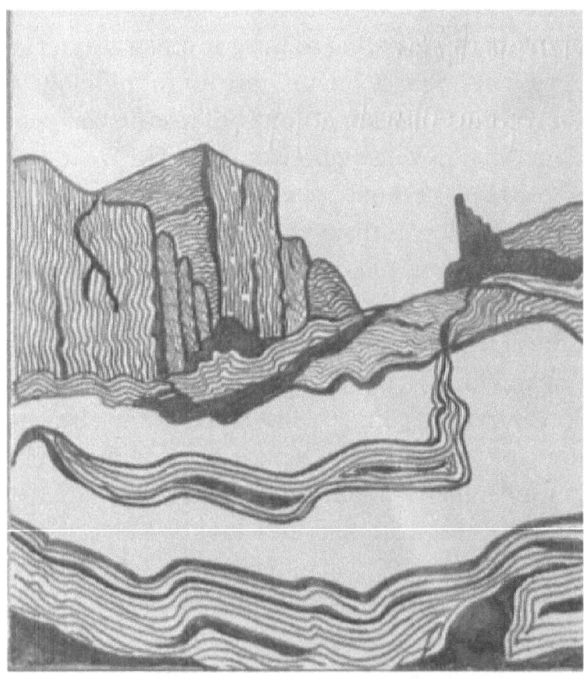

Bohdan's signed, undated, drawing
of undulating serpentine roads leading nowhere

One road seems to be heading toward his desired goal, but a sudden swerve to the right sets it off course. This might easily serve as a visual metaphor for Bohdan's fruitless search for his Ithaca.

Meanwhile, back to Iowa Street, and grampa's cleaning rampages. We were rescued from them in 1967 by an offer to Bohdan from Radio Liberty to head up a Ukrainian division aimed at sending Western information to counter propaganda in Soviet Ukraine. Bohdan accepted the position and went on ahead in late summer. I joined him in October after finding a replacement for my position in the advertising agency where I had been working at the time.

The girls and I were met at the airport in New York by two Bohdans – Rubchak and Boychuk. Because our apartment was still being painted and would not be ready for occupancy for a few days, Boychuk drove us to the motel where he had reserved two rooms for us close to his own home in nearby Rego Park. We settled in on a Monday in late October, prepared to stay until our quarters were ready. On Friday the proprietor informed us that we would have to vacate our rooms, explaining that he needed them for the weekend. It turned out that Boychuk had mistakenly settled us in a house of prostitution – one poet's accommodation selected for another poet's family with their four young daughters! Such a misstep aside, our new life in New York, so full of promise for new experiences and impressions, began in a part of the country where I had long yearned to live.

We spent two years in Forest Hills, enjoying exploring Manhattan, becoming acquainted with Bohdan's friends, entertaining, and most interesting of all, participating in frequent meetings with two prominent Soviet Ukrainian poets, Ivan Drach and Dmytro Pavlychko. They had been sent from Soviet Ukraine to set the misguided diasporans on "the true ideological path." Their mission not only failed, but those "intrepid diasporans" corrupted them to the point that they found themselves in jeopardy upon their return to Kyiv. Although they had anticipated some serious political repercussions, mercifully nothing much came of them. In the meantime, back in New York their KGB "escort" had abandoned his charges and dropped out of sight. We never learned where he went.

Soon after we settled into our new apartment in Forest Hills, Radio Liberty sent Bohdan to Munich for two months. He returned after only one month and discovered that we had survived very well without him. The "other Bohdan" had ensured that our life in New York would continue as before. Bohdan Boychuk had become my steadfast friend and supporter, and so he remained to the end of his life.

In 1969 another move awaited us, this time to New Brunswick, N. J. where Bohdan had been recruited to teach at Rutgers University. Our next three years represented some of the most productive years of our stay on the East Coast. While we maintained our ties with our New York circle, to which we added a New Jersey connection, Bohdan and I also resumed our studies. I graduated with a Phi Beta Kappa BA in 1971, and earned my

M.A. in Intellectual History in 1973, while Bohdan successfully passed his Ph.D. orals that same year, although not without considerable prodding on the part of his mentor John McCormick and me. In 1973 fate took us back to Chicago, where Bohdan had accepted an offer of a professorship in the Slavic Department at the University of Illinois at Chicago. It was destined to become our permanent home, but some of the most troubling years of our marriage also lay ahead.

Backtracking to 1967, Bohdan published "Autumn Romance" in *A Personal Clio*, a poem that appears to harken back to his break with Francesca. The collection *The Radiant Betrayal* might have been seen as a more suitable venue for this poem in light of the time span to which it refers, or, conversely, it could have served as a future projection, in much the same way that "A Recollection of the Moon," written with Francesca in mind but ultimately becoming about me. The most relevant lines from "Autumn Romance" follow:

> Many springs have passed,
> many summers,
> on eternal river reaches the chronicle of branches
> writes changes;
>
> In search of shadows of the past,
> of distant wonders,
> this October I walked every day
> to the autumn woods

A dedicated game player, it is arguable that Bohdan chose to include this poem in *My Personal Clio* as a future projection in time as a way of registering, perhaps only in his own mind, a symbolic message signifying an ending, a closure. This would have emphasized the fact that his love affair with Francesca was now nothing more than an ephemeral dream of a kind that leaves behind only a pleasant memory. Had that pain of unfaithfulness that had haunted him for so long finally lost its edge and given way to a new focus for his love? The only clue to a possible answer that I found was in a letter to me written before our marriage in which he confessed: "I thought that I had two loves in my life. Now I know that there was only one. You" (correspondence now in his archive).

The pattern of Bohdan's ceaseless attempts to "recapture his selfhood," to achieve some reconciliation between his public image and very private inner life had already begun to form back in Chicago in 1963. He wrote then: "It is very difficult to leap over my past and my early promise of a distinguished future. My obsession with death alone seriously impedes my efforts to transcend any failure" (January 16, 1963). As always, he secreted his inner chaos from the prying eyes of the outside world, concealing it behind his masks and word games. His diary entries made it clear that he was in the throes of a relentlessly agonizing inner crisis. Searching for some respite he looked to Winnipeg, and its promise of a new life – new faces, new experiences, some validation of his selfhood. Unfortunately, he did not concede, or perhaps did not yet fully recognize, that the very thing he had left behind in Chicago held at least a partial explanation, needing acknowledgment and the will to change it.

Other concerns also troubled him. He argued in his diary that Ukraine was generously "breastfeeding" its younger poets while ignoring its diaspora "sons." To this Bohdan Boychuk contributed some more personal insights, arguing that Rubchak constantly expected to be "breastfed" by some mother or other, in this case it was "mother Ukraine." Rubchak conceded that Boychuk was probably right but made no serious attempt to change.

Winter was our most memorable season, and January its most special month. In January 1964, we reinforced our final commitment to a lifelong union. After ostensibly insoluble obstructions were resolved the long-awaited event finally took place in snowbound Winnipeg in January a year later. His poetic reference to "the tiny world of eternal January" in "A Wintry Romance," published in the eponymous collection "*A Personal Clio*" validates the special significance of the month. He projected memories of past events onto the future, and poetically reminisced about them as if they had already gone by:

> In a tender battle with snow
> wind wafts in softly and nimbly,
> as though a young lad is welcoming
> his lass at a sky-blue station.
>
> Years will pass, words will become frozen,
> snow flowers will melt.
> Just the memory of You will remain
> the tiny world of eternal January.

In 1973 a final move took us back to Chicago. Bohdan had accepted a professorship at the University of Illinois, where he spent the remainder of his teaching career until retiring in 2005. We lived for some five or six years in adjoining Evanston before moving to Chicago proper, a period still free of those obligations as new property owners that would soon come to traumatize Bohdan. To add to his inner struggle, his mid-life crisis, beginning in 1975, happened when he turned forty. It dragged on for thirteen interminable, stress-filled years, during which our marriage was gravely imperiled.

In 1976 Bohdan made a disastrous real estate purchase that precipitated the first major disaster in our marriage. I have no idea what he was thinking, but he decided to surprise me with the acquisition of a house. Meanwhile, after several weeks of dissertation research on the East Coast I went on to New York to spend a week with Bohdan and Ania Boychuk. During that delightful visit I received a telephone call from Bohdan that began with: "Congratulations, you are now a homeowner!" Without my knowledge he had made a successful bid on that severely rundown building in a transitional neighborhood that we had both rejected earlier. It required a huge cash infusion that we did not have, so much of the labor became our personal obligation. Initially, Bohdan made an attempt to contribute but that came to an end after a number of failed attempts. He retreated from his well-meant efforts into bouts of drinking, then managed even to severely impede my work. One evening, for instance, after I had just finished applying a coat of polyurethane to our freshly sanded floors on the second floor, he arrived home in a state of inebriation and skated happily on my still wet finish, giggling all the while. I don't remember how I reacted to that. My best guess is that it precipitated what Bohdan habitually called "domestic music," involving some of my recently acquired salty language. Unfortunately, more often than not he provoked such scenes, then placed the blame on me.

Contributing to our already imperiled relationship was a harrowing accident the following year suffered by my youngest daughter Stasia. It threatened total blindness and the loss of an eye. Mercifully, this worst prediction did not materialize, but five plastic surgery operations and weeks of uncertainty over the return of her eyesight kept me on edge and, of course, meant a serious loss of dissertation time. I was also teaching two courses as a teaching assistant at the University of Illinois at Chicago. House guests and other visitors contributed welcome diversions, but their visits did create their own pressures. They too added to Bohdan's endless supply of complaints about distractions that allegedly prevented his writing, although they were not the real problem. He could always find things to complain about.

By some miracle we survived these and other traumatizing tribulations, although Bohdan's midlife crisis dragged on until 1988. That year I successfully defended my dissertation. My teaching appointment at Valparaiso, begun two years earlier as a temporary replacement for the chairman of the department who was in China on a research grant, was changed to a tenure-track position. Bohdan continued to write but was never satisfied with what and how much he wrote. Complaints and hyperbolizing notwithstanding, a new collection of poetry appeared in 1980. He released that final collection, *Drowning Marena,* as part of his *The Wing of Icarus* (1980, 1991) volume. For the record I should note some disparity in these dates. In a 1983 diary entry Bohdan wrote that he was hurrying to get the material to the publisher that year, when in fact it had already appeared in 1980. Presumably this was a revised version.

During those troubled mid-life crisis years Bohdan had become more and more obsessed with growing old and dying before he had contributed anything meaningful to his legacy. Much of his poetry reflects this. It was also a time when our relationship was severely eroded, although I hasten to add the fact that those challenges to our staying together were punctuated with incredibly tender moments and demonstrations of affection. Among the most memorable was a poetry reading in Chicago on January 3, 1985, with some 150 listeners in the audience. My eldest daughter Olenka and I sat in the front row. Bohdan's former girlfriend Oksana sat next to her. He stood facing me directly, and without looking away recited "A Song for Mariana" with such intense passion that I was overwhelmed with emotion, and Olenka remarked: "I have never witnessed such an inspiring performance."

Unfortunately, these same years were filled with new pressures. I was "playing contractor" in another recently purchased house in need of major restoration (we had not learned our lesson with the first purchase, although this time contractors did much of the work), teaching and still working on my dissertation. New "domestic music" became a regular feature, for which Bohdan unfairly, and unfailingly, blamed me. Still, there were those rare tender moments as well (October 26, 1985).

Toward the end of Bohdan's mid-life crisis Ukraine's evolving literary process focused on a younger cohort of talented Ukrainian poets who were beginning to gain prominence. The New York Group started losing its readers to these rising young talents, and Bohdan agonized over the future prospects of diaspora writers, together with his own fate as a Ukrainian writer. The beat of his internal crisis went on. He had described it long ago. To repeat: "I would find this so much easier [to bear] if I could achieve some sort of reconciliation with myself." (January 16, 1963). And to repeat: "I now find my masks disgusting. I have played more than enough roles in my life.

It seems as though I have forgotten who I am, yet it is so difficult to forget myself" (July 8, 1963). Obviously that emotion had not lost its edge, while the new literary developments in Ukraine intensified it. In this state of mind he wrote the poem "A Letter to Home." Outwardly he posed the question of the diaspora's literary future, but inwardly it also addressed the parallel state of our own failing relationship:

> So what are we to do? We who exist
> neither in my nor in your future?
> Will we really forever poison with a mug wort potion

(ca 1980)

This next poem, "A Book from Home" appears to have been written at the same time as "A Letter to Home." Bohdan, disgusted with the diaspora literary situation, aimed his sarcasm at the older generation of diaspora readers, who had recently become enamored of all writing coming out of Ukraine, claiming that the New York Group of poets had failed to acquit themselves in charting a new literary direction. Bohdan took exception to this charge with its smug judgment and insisted that the New York Group had acquitted itself very well indeed. By transferring their allegiance to the new literary phenomenon coming out of Ukraine, these ersatz experts were depriving diaspora writers of a readership. He also castigated those same "know it all" diasporans for underrating the works of the older generation of poets in Ukraine. Even if they did not quite rise to the level of progressive innovation, they wrote well and deserved respect. Bohdan's contempt for those misguided "defectors," shedding their crocodile tears, is evident in the first stanza of the poem "A Book from Home":

> Well, really, shoo, hey there, Mykyta:
> a stranger will tell us about everything in the world.
> Muscovite envy and Tatar anger
> are hidden in his crocodile eyes.

In a 1990 televised program from Kyiv titled *Pleiada,* Bohdan unexpectedly requested permission to read two sonnets, to explain: "I would not have written such sonnets today." This reflected his newly formed recognition that Ukraine's literary progress had moved forward as part of a natural course of evolution, even as diaspora writers had found a place in Ukraine's literary development. As I intimated earlier, this was a double-edged sword, however. The poem also functioned as a mask concealing our personal relationship. Bohdan and I were once again beginning to enjoy a mutually affectionate bond (January 30, 1985).

The next poem, "A Mandarin for My Wife," comes from the same collection – *Drowning Marena* (1980, 1991):

> When, having outshined myself,
> like a god, saturated with perpetuity,
> covered in a stone smile,
> I will step onto the edge, the first and last;
>
> curb your crying, and under sweet cherry leaves
> start off alone that roadside day.

Conventional Ukrainian wisdom has it that mandarins (*mandarynky*), or oranges, a scarce and precious commodity at the time, were given to sick people to help speed their recovery. That explains the mandarin in the title. This poem served as a symbol of those healing properties, perhaps offering me hope (apology?) for healing the pain, the grief, that Bohdan knew he sometimes caused me. Or it might suggest that in the event of his passing (he was still obsessed with death) I was not to waste time grieving over what was, but instead I should get on with my new life without him.

Some conjecture leads to the two subjects in the next poem "The Female Saint and the Devil," that Michael Naydan once suggested could easily refer to me and Bohdan. Did Bohdan see himself in the role of the devil? Was this self-reproach an effort to make amends for some feeling of guilt? One diary entry suggests this possibility (November 27, 1989). On November 26, 1989 we attended the wedding of Bohdan's student Irene Horaisky. I was her Matron of Honor while Bohdan played a different role. He drank too much and later spent the entire night at home in a rant against me. In the morning he acknowledged his guilt of the night before, although not spoken directly to me, but written in his diary (November 27): "Poor sleep-deprived Mariana drove to Valparaiso to begin her teaching day. When all is said and done I am a terrible pig!" A few lines later he implied his culpability in provoking our frequent quarrels in a different way: "In such moments I detest myself. Dear God, grant me at least a tiny bit of peace. One has to marvel at Mariana's ability to live with someone like me. But what sort of life is this for her, for us. . ." (November 27, 1989). Expressed poetically it reads:

You're a chambermaid of words and a reaper of mirages.
As though in niches, turned chaff-like yellow,
in your motionless eyes
the wings of doves have turned to stone.

This next poem "Madrigal" is intriguing for its unique structure. Bohdan splits words across two lines, with the separate parts each assuming different meanings. For instance, take the word *polamana*. Bohdan separated it into two words – *pola,* and *mana*; with *pola* hinting at the sexual area under a woman's skirt, and *mana* signifying illusion, or desire. Much of the translation offers more obvious clues to the way that Bohdan deconstructed poetic language, using a method of cubist painters:

Teensily bro
ken is my lady

The beads of her eyes
quiver in mine. The allure
of lips on me.
Trembling.

A snow of touches drift
ed onto dreams –
thinking about the twins
of my lover's body,
so that every cell of my brain

is bathed in its honey.

In the prism of vision
Her shine is shat
tered. In the mélange of night
a dimly lit swarm
of tiny planets:

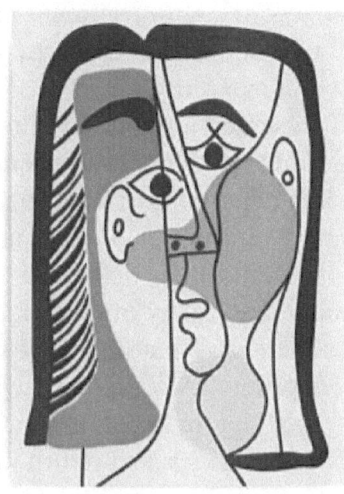

Tete De Femme. Picassso's cubist painting
used as a symbol of Bohdan's poetic deconstruction

I became aware of the poem's existence in 1970 as I was driving us – Vira Vovk, Bohdan and me – to a party at the artist Jurij Solovij's place, I heard him discuss the work with Vira. When I asked to see it, he refused to reveal its title or to tell me where I might find it. As a result I was unaware that he had titled it "Madrigal," and only discovered its whereabouts near the time of his death. It took another year before I was able to understand it in its entirety. The poem is listed under the heading *Eskizy* (brief descriptions, preliminary versions), first published in the initial edition of *Krylo Ikarove* (1980) but likely written earlier. As already suggested, its structure draws on cubist art (December 1965). Bohdan explains the poetic deconstruction as a means of creating a private microcosmic world for the poet (April 8,1965). Further, he went on to a discussion of the literary process in our changing world: "Our society has become so utilitarian that when an artist attempts to exemplify a new reality in his art he does so by deforming his representative image. It appears dreamlike, where the familiar is comingled with the new art form. This creates an illusion of one having once been in such a setting. In reacting to this we feel a negative emotional response that we explain by our dislike of modern art. Why has the artist chosen to represent the new reality by deconstructing old images? The fragments are positioned in a new vision of his world, the details of its existence understood by him alone. The poet invites the viewer to accept the reality of his personal world, one that functions exclusively in accordance with his prescribed laws. This discourse with readers lends itself to a convincing argument for a structural transference of the cubist artistic style to poetry in the form of deconstructed words, each piece bearing a different meaning."

Initially, "December" presented another enigma for me. Why was this particular month chosen for reliving certain memories? Bohdan wrote: "December gives me back my memories" in his poem "Complaining about December." It might be about our romance, one that had begun in September 1963 and continued into December before we were able to consider a final commitment to marry. Too many obstacles, especially my nominal marriage (we had only separated at that juncture) stood in the way of my ability to make a definitive promise. To Bohdan, with his insecurities, this suggested some uncertainty about my commitment to him, a commitment of which he only became aware after his first return in early January 1964. He had already made his own. This will be examined in a different work below. That December he went home to Chicago for Christmas, still unsure, but by the time of his return to Winnipeg my plans had fallen into place, and his anxiety turned to happiness.

> December
> gives me back my memories
> of the state
> of your eyes,
> eyebrows,
> and breasts.
>
> It entices
> with your face

The next poem is a very intense self-examination, written as Bohdan was taking stock of his life. In it he dwells on his wasted youth, his disappointments and failures, and resolutions to turn his life around. We were beginning to settle into a more or less comfortable existence, contrary to his chronic grumbling. As he cast about for solutions to his inner anguish he affirmed once again that so much of it was attributable to his unfortunate upbringing. A series of diary entries (May 26; September 19, October 16, all in 1984; and January 20, 1985) address these problems and imply their source without presenting a solution, or directly naming the source – his mother's manipulation. And somewhat earlier: "At some time in my childhood I lacked the strength to defend myself, to stand up for myself. If I had that strength now, that self-assurance, we would all be much happier. Everything would have fallen into its proper place" (January 26, 1983).

In the first poem he faces himself in a mirror (of his soul?) pleading for forgiveness for his own sin, confessing to having betrayed himself and his talent during his youth by ignoring the unfortunate direction in which his life was clearly heading while there was still time to rescue it from disaster (May 26, 1985). On the eve of the approaching New Year Bohdan made a new resolution (December 31, 1985). He declared his resolve to cultivate some belief in himself, then added an exhortation to cease working against his own interests, to stop allowing himself to be drawn into his own betrayal. Several months later, his resolutions still unrealized, he determined further: "I must engage in less useless longing and spend my time in productive activity" (May 26, 1985). Unfortunately, those resolutions went the way of all the others. The poem "Narcissus" provides an example of his chronic agonizing over the betrayal of his youthful promise, his talent, and his heart (equated with his love of writing), without, in the end, making any changes to his self-destructive behavior:

He pleads before a mirror: "Forgive me!"

again he combs the storage rooms
in his very own masks

And again he enters into an insatiable mirror,
To plead for forgiveness from it again.

He wrote this next poem in response to my own game, calculated to challenge Bohdan's unacceptable behavior toward me on so many occasions. I chose, especially, to retaliate for a "true confession" (a hoax to test me) to an affair with someone named Maria, filled with unlikely details that I spotted only some time later. I might have gone too far in what I did, forgetting his neurotic sensitivity, as his poetic response indicated, but I felt this needed illustrating. Another of the incentives for my retaliation was the fact that Bohdan had the habit of humiliating me during public events. How did he go about all of this? For one example, I fast forward to a future incident, in 1991, when Bohdan was inducted into Ukraine's *Union of Writers* in Kyiv, along with two other Ukrainian-American colleagues. At the investiture ceremony his co-inductees and their wives, together with the Union's leadership, were seated around the ceremonial table. Bohdan steered me to a seat in a far-off corner and told me to sit there. Our friend and Bohdan's fellow poet Ihor Rymaruk noticed this and approached me to inquire why I was seated so far away? I explained that this was Bohdan's wish. Ihor responded by escorting me to the ceremonial table; he pulled up a chair next to Bohdan and declared: "This is where you belong." Bohdan sat there in stony silence and never apologized for his rude behavior.

As for sharing his life and work, it is instructive that he dedicated that fourth collection of poetry – *A Personal Clio* – to me without showing it to me or informing me of its existence. He also wrote a number of poems to and about me, none of which I was aware of during his lifetime. Moved by my suggestive comment and mysterious expression on this particular occasion he wrote:

> What metaphors these are! It's time for me
> to release them in the wind along with Tagore,
>
> because I'm no master of these games, but a slave.
> The most difficult game before me is this:
> whether to cherish or trample flowers –
> to understand you in your entirety.

Here we have his poetic response to my histrionic performance, my "game," aimed at calling attention to the fact that behavior such as his might cut both ways. I was especially interested in retaliating for that cruel hoax. He had already "confessed" to an earlier involvement, with someone he mentioned in the poem "A Book from Home" as his new "diversion." His hoax appears to relate to the same person. For the object of this alleged affair Bohdan chose the name Maria, the middle name of his student named Natalka, with whom he forged a close friendship. This diversion of his evidently gave rise to a fantasy that she pursued with relentless determination, misinterpreting his attentions as the romantic beginning of a permanent attachment. The evidence for this is found in an endless stream of letters filled with her impassioned declarations of love, interspersed with occasional mild rebukes for his failure to take any initiative, or even to call her occasionally. I found with considerable amusement in one of these letters a line "lifted" from Elizabeth Barrett to Robert Browning that read: "I love you Robert. The sound of your voice , the touch of your hand." Natalka repurposed it to read: "I love you Bohdan. The sound of your voice, the touch of your hand." Their close association had its beginning at the start of Bohdan's mid-life crisis, in 1975. He must have reveled in such adoration from a young woman at this critical period in his life. All I actually know about their relationship is found in references in her correspondence to visits to musty bookstores, long walks, and dinners in a restaurant in the Ukrainian neighborhood on Chicago Avenue nicknamed "Zaks." After one such dinner, she wrote a letter in which she declared that the time had come to rethink their reliance on Zaks as a "vinyl crutch" (I have no idea why she used this term), to take their relationship to the next level.

I can only guess at what she meant by the next level, but the next one was closer than she imagined. Her little fantasy had become irritating, so I bundled up a portion of her letters, which Bohdan had left where I could easily find them and mailed them to her with a note indicating that her fantasy, once a source of amusement for me, was now tiresome. Not long afterward, Bohdan informed me that she hoped to pursue a master's program with him, but my objection (that I believe he secretly wanted) caused him to reject her bid so she went on to become a schoolteacher in a distant city instead. In one more letter, describing her new job, and suggesting that they meet during her pending visit to Chicago for "a nice dinner," I found no further reference to Bohdan's young admirer.

I now wish to address his reference to the poet Tagore in "The Hardest Game," as interpreted by Michael Naydan after he translated it (e-mail to me; October 22, 2019): "Tagore revels in [the] feeling of the complete fusion of two inseparable souls. Bohdan seems to be trying to forgive but can't forget "the words' and 'the fiery look.' He can't let go of his rational thoughts and give in to his feelings. . . he wants to feel the way Tagore felt about his beloved. . . but something inside himself holds him back." Was this a double standard, I wondered? An inability to forgive and forget what he believed I meant by my game? It seems that Tagore had left an indelible imprint on Bohdan's emotions, as expressed in Tagore's most famous poem, "Unending Love," and it surely played a part in Bohdan's inability to let me go. He had long been a lover of Tagore's poetry and espouser of his philosophy of indissoluble love, but now exhibited signs of questioning his devotion to those ideals:

> I seem to have loved you in numberless forms, numberless times…
> In life after life, in age after age, forever.
> My spellbound heart has made and remade the necklace of songs,
> That you take as a gift, wear round your neck in your many forms,
> In life after life, in age after age, forever.

In the interest of providing a balanced account of what transpired during those troubled years a brief reference to my own conduct at the time will suggest a possible motive for Bohdan's "confession." I was sharing an affable relationship with my mentor, commencing with our mutual interest in Russian history. I was taking his class at the time. We shared many interests and participated in events related to Russian culture. In Bohdan's mind this close relationship might have seemed more serious than he had imagined. What stood in the way? His references to Tagore, signaling that unbreakable transcendental connection to me, a commitment that went beyond any suggestion of questionable conduct. Then, it seems, my performance raised a doubt in his mind, as I had intended. It left him questioning his devotion to me. Did I share his transcendent love, he mused? Was it time to "release Tagore in the wind." For all of his liberal professions, in the end it seems that there was a double standard in play here. As a woman I was not to be permitted to share the same standard that he enjoyed as a man.

Bohdan's mid-life crisis reached its most extreme level between the years 1981-1986, a segment of our lives during which we were beset by new challenges. These were magnified by his virtually pathological resistance to responsibility, even the thought of which threw him into paroxysms of depression. They coincided with the acquisition of our second run-down property.

The next poem, "Dramaturgy," goes back to Bohdan's concerns articulated in "Letter to Home," where he questions the fate of our future together. I experienced some difficulty understanding this one in the beginning, but I believe that the "life-giving sin" with which he begins represents our early affair in Winnipeg, in 1963, with some feeling of guilt over it because I was still married. In 1975, with the onset of his mid-life crisis, along came his "Theater of Diversions" (Natalka's fantasy) to test his belief in his Tagore-like connection to me. In the end that "Theater" proved to be nothing more than a diversion, a passing distraction for a troubled ego at a critical phase in Bohdan's life. His poetic reference to April coincided with the last day of classes and continuation of our affair in a new set of venues. That autumn must refer to the month of our initial meeting, September, and the onset of our involvement. His new diversion appears to threaten that connection, yet he does not seem serious about a permanent break: "you keep coming and going." In the end I remained a Tagore-like bond:

> I've lived through our lifegiving sin,
> that game of ours, an April and autumn one.
> But you keep coming and going

I already have a new "Theater of Diversions"
For me you
will remain yourself –
the same way I created you.

A series of two-stanza poems under the heading "Compressions," written in the early 1980s, also echo that debilitating crisis phase in Bohdan's troubled life. There are seven separate units in this cycle, of which I will comment on two. It is a kind of summary of those agonizing years of Bohdan's life (1981-1985), which he summarizes as the betrayal of himself, his early promise, his talent, and his heart [love of literature]. During those problematic years he was finally able to face up to the damage to his psyche head on and attribute it directly to his mother's sixteen-years of manipulative behavior (May 26, 1985).

In the first stanza of the first poem in the cycle Bohdan looks back on the promise of his youthful years. The future arrived almost before he knew it, and he realized that he had frittered away that time, together with so many of its possibilities. The second stanza testifies to his regret over this betrayal of "self," the full realization of wasting the precious time that he could never recover:

Once my time used to waft onto me like a brother,
like spring that used to cozy up to me –

Now my time caws at me like a raven,
it roars with laughter in swirling fallen leaves....

When Bohdan turned fifty in 1985 he faced his now shortened literary future by adopting new resolutions in the hope of compensating for some of those lost years. Like all of his previous well-intentioned resolutions, however, the new ones remained on paper. He did continue to write, but there was no gainsaying that the early promise of a brilliant future had been eroded. The damage to his self-assurance had transformed his youthful promise of that future into anxiety over its perceived loss. He now feared venturing too far from his established comfort zone of writing mainly for a Ukrainian audience, without the possibility of rejection. Much later he came to regret this decision but never attempted to rectify it. It also seemed to have become a factor in his habit of resorting to endless streams of excuses for not writing, for not producing, among other things, the two novels that he habitually promised himself. They were never written.

In yet another poem Bohdan turned his attention directly toward me once more. It took him back to our early involvement, to a time before I was able to commit to a permanent relationship. I still felt trapped in a failed first marriage, one that had already caused an attack of psychosomatic paralysis over its hopeless future. Apparently he was unaware at the time of the intensity of my feelings for him, and my desire and determination to find a solution. In December I asked for time not to re-examine my devotion, but to sort things out. My request for time appears to have heightened his sense of insecurity, especially since he had he had already established his own commitment and sought the same assurance on my part:

> I've fashioned a cage of words for you
> to lock you in like a finch.
> I've woven a translucent net of hints
> to capture and forget you.
>
> how could I have known that my words
> have already been serving in your captivity for a while?

In 1983, in his March 23 diary entry he made a key admission. While agonizing over his recurring indebtedness, he mused: "I want to circulate among people (he owed money to so many), I have no wish to sit in a silent corner pitying myself." He brooded over how this might be accomplished, how to free himself spiritually from those demons that haunted him, to return to the self that had been lost somewhere along the way. Two days later he came to a new admission: "Mariana suggested that I had outgrown those endless presentations before limited diaspora audiences in church basements." He appeared to agree, but nothing much changed, and he excused it by rationalizing: "I have no control over my life" (April 28 diary entry).

The turbulent 1980s, with their dramatic highs and lows, slipped into the more tranquil 90s, bringing happier times for both. Bohdan signaled this change at the beginning of the decade with that public confession in Kyiv in 1990, while our family was enjoying a visit to Ukraine together for the first time. Our daughters excitedly witnessed their first public political demonstration on the eve of Ukraine's independence during an annual parade on Khreshchatyk Street marking the beginning of the school year. Journeys to Ukraine were filled with some remarkable (at times unbelievable) episodes. In-flight safety issues also became a focus. As illustrated by a now Ukrainian-speaking cabin attendant with an announcement that she would not point out safety features because none of them worked. That return trip was interesting for other reasons as well. A new friend in Kyiv had given my daughters a large jar of *varenyky* (potato dumplings). Clearly they would not have cleared customs so Olenka began distributing them to our fellow passengers. For their part, our Ukrainian travel companions opened their briefcases, out of which they disgorged bottles of vodka; our "happy hour" commenced. It was 8:00 a.m. so I questioned this generous act. Their reply was to remind us that elsewhere in various parts of the world it was already afternoon.

In the summer of 1993, the year of Bohdan's final journey to Ukraine, an unexpected disaster loomed. Bohdan's mother experienced a fall while he and I were spending several weeks in Ukraine. Upon our return we visited her in the hospital, and as it happened her doctor (Bandura) was there, considering the possible need for an operation to correct something in her pelvis that he thought might not have healed properly. When he suggested this I turned to him in horror with: "This is an 88-year-old woman with a bad heart. Can she withstand such a trauma?" His response? "Who told you she has a bad heart?" I glanced meaningfully in *mamusia's* direction and noticed a sick grin on her face (the kind referred to colloquially by young people as "a shit-eating grin"). Unfortunately, this experience so traumatized Bohdan that he never again journeyed to Ukraine, or indeed even ventured out of the country except for brief visits to Canada. He refused to discuss his reasons. Trips to Canada involved visits to my parents in Saskatoon. They resulted in some amusing episodes of their own, but that is a discussion for a different time.

Returning to the problem at hand: despite my accidental revelation of the fiction of a bad heart, when *mamusia* was discharged from the hospital I foolishly invited her to stay with us until she regained her strength. She happily settled into our Chicago home with her son and promptly exhibited no sign of leaving. Her first suggestion was to have us remove and store our furniture in the basement to make room for her thrift-store pieces. I was spending each week in Valparaiso, leaving Bohdan to minister to her, and left the solution to him. When I arrived on the first Saturday of the new arrangement, laden with heavy bags of their groceries, she intercepted me on the exterior stairs with a carefully staged "vinchuvannia" a traditional Ukrainian holiday greeting serving as an invitation into someone's home. Bohdan looked on with amusement while I was left holding the bag(s). Three weeks later *mamusia* approached Bohdan with a newly-crafted proposition – the two of them would live together as they had in the past. "What about Mariana?"

Bohdan asked innocently. "Where would she live?" "In Indiana of course," was *mamuisia*'s instant response. Bohdan pursued this farce in ostensible earnestness. "Are you suggesting that I divorce her?" He asked innocently. "If necessary," she replied solemnly. "Then where would we live? "Why, here, of course," she replied. "Here?" Not prepared to end this game just yet, Bohdan continued with: "Can you come up with a good reason why Mariana should turn over a house that her parents paid for (they helped substantially) so that you and I might enjoy it without her?" he asked. That stumped her, but she soon went to work on an alternate scheme.

Before she could craft a new stratagem, a now desperate Bohdan enlisted the help of our friend Lesia Kochman to arrange for *mamusia*'s transfer to a nearby nursing home where Lesia's own mother was living. I arrived in Chicago on November 23 en route to present a paper in Honolulu. Bohdan immediately intercepted me and insisted that I drive his mother to the nursing home, to which I explained that I had an early morning flight and needed time to pack. "Buy yourself an entire wardrobe in Hawaii, only take her there now," was his frantic answer. We transported *mamusia* to the nursing home to the refrain of: "my son would never do this to me." Naturally, I became the villain by default, a role I happily (not to say gratefully) accepted. Two years later the unheard of happened. Perhaps for the first time in its history the director of the nursing home telephoned a client demanding that he take his mother back. In her call to Bohdan she explained that his mother was disruptive and unmanageable."Out of the question," Bohdan responded, so at the home they "manufactured" (I am convinced it was a ruse) a life-threatening brain disease that required immediate surgery. A young doctor just out of medical school blithely assured Bohdan that he "could cure her." Without seeking a second opinion, an alarmed Bohdan assented to the operation, out of which his mother emerged in a virtually comatose state. She was dispatched to a distant surgical center, hooked up to machines that breathed for and fed her for five long years. Bohdan never mentioned her again

No longer threatened with separation we now enjoyed our time together, theater, the symphony, parties, and the like. In 2005 Bohdan retired from the classroom; we decided to move to New Jersey to be closer to our daughters and their growing families. Bohdan moved first and I followed in 2006. We got off to a good start, with Bohdan continuing to write, and enjoying some pleasing entertaining with interesting people, but he did not adapt well to life on the East Coast. Several years after our arrival he declared, in his inimitable way: "Ia skvituvav" (I quit). And he did, with a vengeance. The last large public function he attended was at Shevchenko Scientific Society in New York City in 2011 – my 80th birthday celebration, combined with the launch of the first of my two edited and translated collections on Ukrainian women. His own book, titled *Myths of Metamorphoses. or Searching for The Good World,* a volume of his selected essays translated from English into Ukrainian, was published in Lviv a year later.

On September 18, 2018, fifty-five years to the day from our first meeting, we took Bohdan to the nearby Denville Hospital Emergency Room. On September 23, 2018, fifty-five years from the moment of our unspoken commitment to each other in that university elevator, tragically he passed out of my life into eternity.

My intent here has been to illuminate certain aspects of Bohdan's extremely complex poetry, basing my commentaries primarily on poems with some connection to or about me, in the knowledge that no literary critic is in a position to do so because only I possess the archival resources to accomplish this. His diaries, correspondence, and manuscripts left behind, most of which I was able read for the first time, helped me get to know so much better a husband with whom I had lived for so long and knew so little. I was always aware that Bohdan was a very private person, but I did not fully recognize how jealously he guarded that privacy. My new insights and enhanced acquaintance with this enigmatic man have also helped me to offer, for further study, a more nuanced picture of his private world of poetry and his psychological state while writing. There is still a great deal left to be plumbed in Bohdan's house of poetic mirrors, but it is hoped that my modest contribution will provide at least some helpful new insights and contribute to a fuller appreciation of the work of this talented, erudite, and inscrutable poet. For scholars wishing to conduct further research on his works, to enhance what is already known or guessed at, that material will be found in his archive (known as the Bohdan and Mariana Rubchak Archive), housed at the Bakhmeteff Archival collection of the New York Group of Poets at Columbia University. His correspondence and manuscripts have already been made available. I will release the remainder of the materials, most importantly his diaries, as soon as I am done working with them. On a final note, this has been a labor of love for a multitalented man who despite his prickly personality gave and received much love.

AFTERWORD II

THE COMPLEXITY AND PERPLEXITY OF BOHDAN RUBCHAK: REMARKS ON TRANSLATING HIS POETRY

Svitlana Budzhak-Jones

Translating poetry, in general, is not an easy task. Conveying rhymes, rhythms, sound effects, and meaning into another language is very challenging. The more distant the languages are, the more demanding the task. Translating Bohdan Rubchak's poetry is further exacerbated by the poet's unique, somewhat surrealistic writing style. Emigré Ukrainian poet Bohdan Rubchak loves to combine all those emblematic features of poetry with free word order, pushing the language boundaries of Ukrainian to extremes. Transferring the meaning as well as preserving all the stylistic features becomes an almost irresolvable task. Ukrainian and English differ significantly in grammar and sound forms. Ukrainian is an Eastern Slavic language, highly inflectional, fusional, with free word-order. English is a Germanic language. It is mostly analytical, with considerably restricted word-order. Ukrainian allows the poet to experiment with creating various rhyme and sound patterns without being restricted by the word order. In turn, the translators are faced in many instances with the dilemma whether to transfer the meaning of the poem as truthfully to the original as possible, or to preserve the rhyme, or to recreate the sound patterns, or to maintain the rhythm. Preserving more than one of those features in a translated version of Rubchak's poems proved to be next to impossible. The translators were guided by the principle of transferring the meaning of the poem as a paramount goal. The rest was secondary and to be preserved or replicated whenever possible. The following illustrate how we as translators fulfilled those tasks.

Our primary task of transferring the meaning of Bohdan Rubchak's poems turned out to be complicated on multiple levels, but incredibly rewarding intellectually. Deciphering the poet's message does not come easy because of the multiple masks, both linguistic and symbolic, that he employs in his poetry that some critics have described as surrealistic. The poet's intended meaning is not always apparent at first reading. He plays with Ukrainian free word order and polysemic lexemes undauntedly and unconventionally. Word order entanglements, exemplified in (1) from "Three Emblems," are very frequent in his poetry, attesting to his masterful manipulation of the Ukrainian language.

До неба зводить руки (Three Emblems) (1)
[To sky raises arms]

Тополі позив високий.
[Of poplar calling high].

Word for word literal translation (here after shown in square brackets) is not very helpful in such cases. It takes some detective work to establish the meaning and convert it to the word order required by English grammar. Since the only verb here is marked for singular, the subject is not difficult to find. The only noun marked for singular Nominative case is *позив* [pozyv] "calling." The adjective following it *високий* [vysokyi] "high" is also in the singular Nominative, and the gender of these two words is identical, i.e. masculine. Hence, the latter modifies the former, creating the noun phrase "high calling" and serves as the subject phrase, i.e. "High calling raises." The direct object here is most likely *руки* [ruky] "arms/hands" since it is in Accusative case required by the verb and there is no other candidate for it. The indirect object *до неба* [do neba] "to sky" will follow the direct object, giving us roughly the following: "High calling raises hands/arms to sky." The puzzle here is the noun *тополі* [topoli] "(of a) poplar." It could be related to *ruky* "arms/hands," as in "hands/arms of poplar," or it could be part of the subject "high calling", as in "high calling of poplar." The poet places the noun "poplar" in a strategic location immediately following the noun "hands/arms" and immediately preceding the noun "calling." This suggests double association of the noun "poplar" with both the preceding and the following words. Since such word ordering is not allowed in English, the translators obviated it by using a word in one instance and inserting its pronoun in another. This gave us the following translation skeleton in (2):

High calling of poplar (2)
raises its hands/arms to sky

The next step is to convert it into literary English by adding articles (which do not exist in Ukrainian), choosing only one word from "hands/arms" (since the word in Ukrainian means both), and replacing some words with synonyms in order to make it more poetic. This is the part where the knowledge of a native English speaker is invaluable. Our final translation of this verse took the following shape in (3):

The high calling of a poplar tree (3)
stretches its arms to the sky.

There are two noticeable features in the original: the sound pattern (i.e., *zvodyt', pozyv, vysokyi*) and the rhyming of both lines (i.e., *ruky – vysokyi*). The translators were able to approximate some sound patterning (i.e., **stretches its arms to the sky**) by substituting "stretching" for "raising." However, the rhyme was not possible to replicate without changing the meaning.

Enthusiastic experimentation with free word order is very frequent in Rubchak's poetry. It leads to some instances when grammar rules cannot govern the relationship between the words in a sentence. It is the meaning then that makes the final call in our decision of how to translate a particular line or verse. Consider, for example, the following in (4):

і заховаєш у лахміття бруд (An Evening Prayer) (4)
[and (you-singular) will hide into rags dirt]]

This sentence should be rendered into normative English as "You will hide dirt in the rags." However, it makes no sense in the poem. The preceding lines (shown in (5)) suggest something different. Someone will be given a "reward," will give thanks for it, and then will hide it "in the dirt of rags," giving us the opposite of what the grammar would have dictated. The poet stretches the prepositional phrase moving the preposition "in" away from the head noun "dirt" which it should immediately precede and inserts the object "rags" which should follow the noun instead. This is when the intuitive understanding of a native Ukrainian speaker has proven to be of great consequence. Our final translation is shown in (5) below:

Я дам тобі за твій нечистий труд   (An Evening Prayer)   (5)
цих кілька слів. Подякуєш нещиро
і заховаєш у лахміття бруд.

I'll give you these several words for your
ungodly labor. You'll thank me insincerely
and bury them in the dirt of rags.

The extensive and clever use of polysemic nouns also contributes to the complexity of understanding and transferal of the correct meaning from Ukrainian into English. Sometimes, the translators had to make their best guess regarding the author's intended meaning, as in (6), for example:

Віє спальнями **пах** помад   (Chopin)   (6)
[(It) blows (through) bedrooms crotch/smell (of) lipsticks]

This one line presents three different problems for translation. The first one is related to the noun *пах* [pah]. In Ukrainian this noun could mean three things: 1) a crotch; 2) smell/scent, shortened from the noun *запах* [zapah]; and 3) the sound of a shooting gun. While the last meaning would be irrelevant here, either of the former two meanings could be implied. There may be a correlation between "bedrooms" and "crotch," but because of the verb *віє* [viye] "blows, winds" we decided that it is more likely that the second meaning (i.e. smell/scent) is intended here. This gives us the rough meaning of "the scent of lipstick blows through the bedrooms."

The second puzzlement is associated with the noun *помад* [pomad]. In Ukrainian it could mean two things: 1) pomade, a smooth oily substance rubbed on skin or hair as a cosmetic or for medicinal purposes; 2) same type of substance applied to lips, lipstick. Either meaning could be equally applied in this context. Instead of using both words, we decided to omit it altogether. Instead, we chose to use the word "scent" rather than "smell" for *"pah."* The former encompasses several meanings including the meaning of a pleasant smell, perfume, and a pleasant-smelling liquid applied to skin. It would refer to both words in Ukrainian, i.e. "pah" and "pomad."

AFTERWORDS

The third ambiguity comes from the noun *спальнями* [spal'niamy] "bedrooms" in the Instrumental case. It could mean either "by bedrooms" or "through/via bedrooms", i.e. the scent may smell like bedrooms or the scent is spread through the bedrooms. After deliberation we choose to go with the former. When the meaning is finally established, the translation takes the following shape in (7):

The scent gives off the air of bedrooms. (7)

The bold experimentation with free word order and polysemy in Ukrainian are not the only challenges of Rubchak's poetry. New word creations add to the complexity of interpretation of meaning. The author uses innovative ways of creating new words, proving that the Ukrainian language is a living entity full of surprises and revelations. Consider, for instance, the following example from the poem "A Flash and a Reflection" in (8):

У смерти скрученім **струнні**   (A Flash and a Reflection)   (8)
[In death twisted string-like/by strings]

Затерпли звуки безлунні –
[Got numb sounds echoless]

Untangling the syntax of the phrase *У смерти скрученім струнні* [U smerty skruchenim strunni] is in itself a fascinating experience for a translator. The preposition *у* [u] "in/at" should be immediately adjacent to the noun/noun-phrase it governs. In the above sentence the preposition is immediately preceding *smerty* "death" (singular, feminine, prepositional/genitive case?) suggesting that we could be dealing with the phrase *u smerty* "in death/at death." The following word *skruchenim* "twisted" is an adjective in the prepositional case, which could also be in the same case as the preceding word. However, it has a different gender, i.e. masculine/neuter. Hence, it does not refer to the preceding feminine noun "death." Could it modify the following word *strunni* "string-like/by strings?" But the latter appears to have an adjectival form in the plural, different in number from the preceding word. It rhymes with the word *безлунні* [bezlunni] "echoless" at the end of the next line, which is definitely an adjective in the plural. This points to the fact that *strunni* "string-like/by strings" could be an adjective in the plural form, modifying the same noun as *bezlunni* "echoless" in (9):

струнні звуки – безлунні звуки, (9)
"string sounds" – "echoless sounds"

But this cannot be correct. In the first line the adjective *skruchenim* "twisted" is then left out without the noun it modifies. The clue to resolve this dilemma comes from the following lines below (shown in (10)).

Не вчує **його** білокорий (10)
[(It) won't hear **him/it** white-crusted]

потік, що німує нині
[stream, that is being numb today]

The pronoun *його* [yoho] "him/it" refers to something masculine or neuter in gender above. The only candidate for it is *strunni* "string-like" if we assume that it is not an adjective, as originally implied. It appears to be a newly created noun *струння* [strunnia] ("strings" in a collective form). The word does not exist in modern Ukrainian. The poet created it by analogy with similar collective nouns (e.g., *насіння* [nasinnia] "seeds," *бадилля* [badyllia] "tops of plants," *колосся* [kolossia] "ears of wheat," etc.). It is used in the prepositional case, singular, neuter gender, and it matches perfectly well with the modifier "twisted." They create a noun phrase with the preposition *у* [u] "in/at," even though it is not immediately adjacent to the them, i.e. *u […] skruchenim strunni* "in twisted strings." The noun *smerty* "death" must then not be in the prepositional but in the genitive case, i.e. "of death," giving us the following skeleton to work with: "in twisted strings of death." This leads to the final translation of (8) shown in (11):

in the crumpled strings of death (11)
echoless sounds grew numb, –

Similarly, the poet creates the noun *сіття* [sittia] "nets/network" in "A Song for Mariana" in (12), and the noun *хустя* [hustia] "kerchiefs" in "A Flash and a Reflection" in (13). The former is derived from the noun *сіть* [sit'] "net" and the latter from the noun *хустка* [khustka] "kerchief" to make collective neuter nouns in the singular.

мов зливи **сіття** (12)
"like torrents of nets"

не випере синє **хустя**	(13)
"(It) won't wash the blue scarves"	

Rubchak plays with Ukrainian words like a craftsman with mosaic beads, creating new forms and meanings. The adjective *розсріблений* [rozsriblenyi] also does not exist in Ukrainian. It is compounded from two perfectly legitimate parts: the prefix *роз-* [roz-] denoting separation, disruption, expansion, and the adjective *сріблений* [sriblenyi] "silver-covered." The translators inferred that Rubchak's *розсріблена радість* [rozsriblena radist'] refers to "joy sprinkled with silver." After figuring out the meaning, the final translation took the form of "silver beads of joy."

Збираю **розсріблену** радість	(A Song for Mariana)	(14)
"(I) gather silver beads of joy"		

Rubchak uses various techniques to create new words. One of his methods entails seamlessly fusing two existing words into a new compound. This allows him to maintain rhythm and craft unique poetic expressions such as those in (15 and 16). His poems abound with such creations. And even though they are new and unusual for a Ukrainian reader, they are not difficult to replicate in English. In some cases, they seemed like calques from English, e.g. *козошкірим* [kozoshkirym] "goatskin" in (15).

під вітрилом **козошкірим**	(An Evening Prayer)	(15)
"under a **goatskin** sail"		

In many other instances his new creations were unusual in English, as well, but they mapped seamlessly into their English counterparts without any changes or substitutions such as the ones in (16) – (20). Sometimes, however, we had to paraphrase one Ukrainian word as two or three words in English. For example, *первобажання* [pervobazhannia] was translated as the "first desire" in "The Wing of Icarus," and *щедробарвно* [shchedrobarvno] as "rich in colors" in "In a Room of a Hundred Mirrors."

Крилоокий Ікар	(A Windy Icarus)	(16)
"a **wing-eyed** Icarus"		

Синьодугасті тіні	(Ars Poetica)	(17)
"**blue-arched** shadows"		

Столапим тропам	(To Clio)	(18)
"for **hundred-pawed** trails"		
Білоустий спогад	(November)	(19)
"a **white-lipped** recollection"		
Звуколезий ніж	(Chopin)	(20)
"the **sound-bladed** knife"		

On rare occasion we as translators have had to imitate the author and create a new compound in English, as in the case of Rubchak's adverb *м'якостопо* [m'iakostopo] in "The Wing of Icarus." It consists of two words *м'яко* [m'iako] "softly" and *стопо* [stopo] "sole/footstep[-like]." We decided to imitate the poet and create a similar adverb in English, i.e., "softsteppingly."

There are cases when the meaning of the newly created word remains ambiguous no matter what we do or look at. The adjectival participle *переполовілі* [perepolovili] in (21) comprises the root of the noun *полова* [polova] "chaff, husk" and the prefix *пере-* [pere-] "over/ across/ through." It could mean several things, i.e. 1) aged, 2) rotted-like chaff, or 3) turned a chaff-like color in time. The translators decided to go as close to the text as possible and leave it to the reader to decipher the meaning.

в нішах переполовілих	(The Female Saint and the Devil)	(21)
"in niches, turned chaff-like yellow"		

Sometimes we had to omit some information. This is usually the case when the Ukrainian animate noun is marked for feminine gender. Consider, for example, two nouns in (22). Both of them are overtly marked as feminine gender. We could have added additional information in English by inserting a "woman," "female," or "she." But that would make the line too bulky. The translators decided to omit this information altogether because the second noun consisted of a noun "birthgiver." By default, it would entail the connotation of feminine gender in English.

Безвірниця – Світородиця	(And Then We Rode Home)	(22)
"Non-believer - World Birthgiver"		

"Svitorodytsia" is formed on the basis of the noun "Bohorodytsia" (literally: Birthgiver of God), the name for the Blessed Virgin in Ukrainian. In another instance we had no choice but to insert additional information in the translation because leaving it without the specific feminine marker would lead to mistranslation. In the title of the poem in (23) the noun *Свята* [sviata] refers to a female saint. Leaving it unmarked for feminine gender would suggest masculine gender by default, reinforced by the second noun in the title *чорт* [chort] "devil." The latter is typically masculine and would transfer masculine gender by analogy to the former. Hence, the translation of "the female saint."

Свята і чорт (23)
"The Female Saint and the Devil"

Interestingly, the noun *Sviata* is polysemic in Ukrainian. It can also mean "holidays." Without additional context we could have mistranslated it. However, the entire meaning of the poem describes an icon. One could argue that the icon infers religious holidays. But additional knowledge of knowing that the poet privately discussed an icon of a female saint fighting a devil, known as *Margaret of Antioch* in the West, and *Saint Marina the Great Martyr* in the East, gave the translators confidence that the title is about a female saint.

The poet loves playing not only with words but with sounds, as well. Consider the title of the poem *Блиск і відблиск* [Blysk i vidblysk] "Shine and reflection." The author uses two closely related words with similar phonemes to express opposite phenomena: one emits light while the other just reflects it. The translators worked with both words (i.e., shine and reflection) to find antonyms with similar phonemics in English. "Shine" did not produce a desired result. But we were lucky to find such dichotomy for the word "reflection." Hence, the English title: "A Flash and a Reflection."

Sometimes the desired dichotomy does not appear to exist in Ukrainian. The poet then stretches language constraints to arrive at the intended duality. Consider words *звинно* [zvynno] "with guilt" and *безвинно* (bezvynno) "without guilt" from "A Book from Home." The latter one, a modern Ukrainian adverb, consists of the prefix *без-* [bez-] "without" and *винно* [vynno] "guilty," i.e. "without guilt." The poet needed the antonym derived from the same root to mean "with guilt." He could not just drop the prefix bez- ("without"), because the adverb "vynno" in the meaning of "guilty", is not used in Ukrainian. In fact, in dialectal speech (i.e. in Hutsul, a Western Ukrainian dialect of the Carpathians) it could mean "sourly." To remedy the problem, the poet simply adds the Ukrainian prefix *з-* ([z-] "with") and creates a new adverb *zvynno* ("with guilt").

The poet is very inventive. He creates new, nonexistent words from very common words and word-forming affixes. Consider the noun *розстріли* [rozstrily] in (24). At first glance a translator can be misled by the homonymous noun formed from the verb *розстріляти* "to execute by firing squad." But this is a poem about Mozart. Execution makes no sense here. The noun in question is used in association with the noun *листка* [lystka] which could mean either "of a leaf" or "of a small [paper] sheet." In connection to a leaf, it suddenly makes sense. A leaf has arrows or *стріли* [strily], typically used in the diminutive form *стрілки* [strilky]. Rubchak adds the prefix *роз-* [roz-] denoting separation, disruption, expansion and acquires the new meaning of "dispersing of arrows." In order to translate it into English we had to expand the phrase by adding additional words to describe the intended meaning:

В **розстрілах** листка (Mozart) (24)
"In the bursting arrows of leaf veins"

Rubchak's repertoire is also rich in loans and borrowings from other languages. *Безлунні* [bezlunni] "echoless" from "A Flash and a Reflection" comes from Russian "луна/лунный" [luna/lunnyi] "echo." The Ukrainian verb *лунати* [lunaty] "to sound" does not have an adjectival form. So, the poet creates one by borrowing it from Russian and adding the Ukrainian prefix *без-* [bez-] "without" to it. Other examples of Russian borrowings are the adjective *безконечний* [bezkonechnyi] "infinite" and the verb *обожає* [obozhaie] "adores" in "The Gods." Ukrainian equivalents of those words are *безкінечний* [bezkinechnyi], and *обожнює* [obozhniuye] correspondingly. The knowledge of other languages for translators proved to be advantageous.

In "My Ithaca" the poet borrowed the noun *путі* [puti] "paths/roads" from Russian. The Ukrainian equivalent for it should be *шлях* [shliah]. However, for the sound pattern (shown in (25)) the Russian one fit better. Moreover, it sounds similar to the Ukrainian noun *пута* [puta] "manacles" which could be inferred by association with the following verb *опутали* [oputaly] "to manacle/to entangle." One may argue that the poet just misspelled the noun *putí* instead of *púta*. But we decided that the poet used the Russian noun *puti* intentionally. It gave him the meaning he intended, as evidenced from the previous line (i.e. leaving desires, leaving homes, going somewhere, being on the road). And at the same time, it echoed the verb *oputaly*. This double entendre was difficult to reproduce in English. We solved the dilemma by creating a compound in English "manacle-paths" in line with the poet's creativity in Ukrainian.

> Лишав багато бажань, домів, –   (My Ithaca)   (25)
> **путі** опутали тіло.
>
> I was leaving behind many desires and many homes –
> manacle-**paths** ensnared the body.

Several lines later in the same poem the poet used the noun *путь* [put'] "road/path" (shown in (26)), i.e. the singular form of the earlier version *puti*. This confirmed our assumption that *puti* in (25) is not a misspelling, but an intentional use of the Russian loanword to create a double meaning.

> Сваволя плавань тепер – полон,   (My Ithaca)   (26)
> а **путь** полинова, тьмава.
>
> Now the free will of sailing is – captivity,
> and a wormwood **path** and gloom.

Interestingly, the Russian noun *put'* "road" is of the masculine gender. The poet borrows it and fully integrates it into Ukrainian assigning the feminine gender to it, which is attested by its two modifiers *полинова* [polynova] "wormwood" and *тьмава* [t'mava] "gloomy", both in the feminine gender.

One of the most fascinating examples of using a Russian borrowing in Ukrainian is shown in (27):

> В калейдоскопі, пишнім **позолотою**,   (To Clio)   (27)
> промигнеш у кількох ярких фігурах,
> а потім час, як сніг хрести на горах,
> увінчить бюсти вічністю **золатою**.
>
> In a kaleidoscope, sumptuous with gilding,
> you will flash in several bright figures,
> and then time, like snow crowning crosses on the mountains,
> will crown the busts with ash-covered eternity.

The poet needed a word meaning "ash-covered" but close in sound, form, and rhyme to the Ukrainian word *позолота* [pozolóta] "gilding" in the first line. He created an entirely new word based on the Russian noun *зола* [zolá] "ash." The Ukrainian equivalent for it would have been *попіл* [pópil]. He could have created a new word from it to rhyme with *pozolota*, something like, for example, *попелята* [popeliáta], but it would have been lacking in sound similarity with the rhyming noun *pozolota*.

Borrowings from English also are scattered throughout Rubchak's poems. The poet incorporates words of English origin into Ukrainian grammar with ease and mastery. The majority of these borrowings are nouns, as illustrated in (28)-(30):

маєстатом [mayestatom] — majestic (A Recollection of the Moon) (28)
скаль [skal'] — scales (Mozart) (29)
строкар [strokar] — stroker (Don Juan) (30)

Other parts of speech derived from English are much less plentiful, but they still occur. Consider the adjective *брокатний* [brokatnyi] in "December." There is no such a word in the Dictionary of Modern Ukrainian. However, its root can be easily connected to the English noun "brocade." Translating such words back into English was not that difficult, but it was very interesting to observe the poet's incorporation of such words into Ukrainian. This is not surprising since the author lived in the English-speaking world most of his life. What is surprising, that his poems did not have many more of such borrowings from English considering that he grew up, received his education and resided all his adult life in an English-speaking environment.

Rubchak's command of Ukrainian is extremely impressive. His lexical repertoire is very rich in rarely used words. He includes a great deal of uncommon and archaic nouns and forms in his Ukrainian poems which may prove to be a challenge even for a native Ukrainian speaker. Some examples are given in (31)-(36):

хижі **чоти** (To Clio) (31)
"predatory formations"

гладить **рінь** прибій (Mozart) (32)
"the surf smooths sand gravel"

карколомним спритом (A Book from Home) (33)
"by dazzling deftness"

клали з **лиликів** шкіри "piled up skins from bats"	(Drowning Marena)	(34)
часу **згагою** "the parchedness of time"	(Drowning Marena)	(35)
Трачі жбурнуть на пили **шваргома** "lumbermen will hastily toss you onto saws"	(Compressions)	(36)

Another challenge in translating Rubchak's poetry comes from his use of dialectal speech. He skillfully blends single dialectal words and incorporates syntactic constructions. Consider the following examples. In (37) literary Ukrainian one would say *снитися* [snytysia] "to dream+Reflexive" or *побачити уві сні* [pobachyty u vi sni] "to see in a dream." Rubchak instead uses the dialectal verb *снити* [snyty] "to dream", used in several Western Ukrainian dialects, which functions by analogy to its English counterpart, the verb *to dream*.

Ніким недосягнене **виснити** "For dreaming out what no one had achieved"	(A Windy Icarus)	(37)

One of the tricky examples of the poet's incorporation of dialectal speech appears in (38) from "A Flash and a Reflection." The preposition *про* [pro] in literary Ukrainian means "about," rendering the following translation "to wash blue scarves about the green holidays." This makes no sense. However, in dialectal speech, especially among the Hutsuls from the Ukrainian Carpathian Mountains, the preposition *про* [pro] may also mean "for," as in *про святки* [pro sviatky] "for the holidays" or *про всєк випадок* [pro vsiek vypadok] "just in case." It is most likely that the poet uses this preposition in the meaning of "for" in the context of (38). The translation thus makes sense with this adjustment. This is a case when the knowledge of dialectal speech is inevitably very helpful for the translators.

йому, **про** зелені свята, не випере синє хустя.	(A Flash and a Reflection)	(38)
to it **for** the green holidays, (it) won't wash the blue scarves		

Another brainteaser for translators comes from Rubchak's fluid syntactic boundaries. By making them undefined the author creates ambiguity. This provides the reader with more discretion and makes the job of a translator more challenging. In (39), for example, the verb *стануть* [stanut'] "will become" may take one noun for a subject, i.e. "suits of armor," or two, i.e. "suits of armor" and "gonfalons," or three, "suits of armor," "gonfalons," and "crowns," or even four, i.e. "suits of armor," "gonfalons," "crowns," and "wounds of the host." On the other hand, the subject of the coordinate clause *цвіль* [tsvil'] "mold" may take any number of direct objects above it, from one, i.e. "runes of victory," to four, i.e. "runes of victory," "wounds of the host," "crowns," and "gonfalons." Knowing the poet's propensity for word order experimentation, all options are possible. For the purpose of our translation we split this sentence in two concurrent clauses at the conjunction site with the impartial meaning.

Гніздом щурів, червивою державою   (To Clio)   (39)
кольчуги стануть, корогви, корони,
і раті рани, перемоги руни
зрівняє цвіль байдужістю іржавою.

Suits of armor, gonfalons, crowns
will become a nest of rats, a worm-eaten state,
and the mold of rusty indifference will raze
wounds of the host, the runes of victory.

One of Rubchak's most stylistically challenging poems is "A Madrigal." It is deceptively simple. But the more one reads it, the more one realizes how convoluted and perplexing it is. The poem starts with seemingly straightforward meaning (see in [40]). An average casual reader may understand this as something like "my lady lures me in a tiny skirt." However, the lines that follow, reveal the poet's secret. The reader's first impression fails to convey the intended meaning. On closer examination of the lines, the reader can see that the poet splits words into two parts across lines. Each part can exist on its own suggesting one meaning. When those parts of the word are read together as one word, the meaning changes drastically. For example, the word *пола* [pola] "skirt, lap, flap" at the end of the first line and the word *мана* [mana] "appeal/appealing, allure/alluring" at the beginning of the second line, guide the reader to the meaning stated above. But when those two words are written together, another meaning emerges: i.e. *поламана* [polamana] "broken."

| Крихітно пола | (A Madrigal) | (40) |

[Tiny-like skirt/lap]

мана моя дама.
[alluring my lady]

The poem presents several similar puzzles with double meaning. Unfortunately, the translators were not able to preserve the double entendre in the offered translation. That was a clear case of being "lost in translation." However, we tried to preserve the playfulness and sentiment, as in (41).

Teensily bro (41)
ken is my lady.

Rubchak's kaleidoscopic language does not bypass truly Ukrainian idioms either. Translating such expressions from one language to another is always a challenge. In "A Book from Home" Rubchak uses the verb *бандурить* [banduryt']. It is derived from an expression "to strum on a bandura" (a traditional Ukrainian string instrument) and it figuratively refers to doing nothing important, talking idly, telling nonsense, etc. The translators had to replace the Ukrainian idiom with a comparable English one. "To make chin music" would have the closest meaning, but it has no reference to a string instrument. Hence, we decided on the translation in (42):

Хай не **бандурить** нам (A Book from Home) (42)
"May he not strum to us"

Comprehending Rubchak's poetry to the finest detail is essential for proper translation. It requires deciphering the intended meaning with a certain amount of detective work that encompasses following the modifier-noun and noun-verb relations based on case, number, and gender endings; then making the logical conclusion based on those findings and common sense. It helped tremendously to have a team of two translators. One of us is a native English speaker, while the other's mother tongue is Ukrainian with the intimate knowledge of Western Ukrainian dialects. The profound knowledge of both Ukrainian and English grammar, as well as Ukrainian dialectal traditions were inevitably very advantageous. Translating Rubchak's poems is no small task. It is both fascinating and intellectually rewarding. When one considers the poet's bold stretching of syntactic and phonological boundaries, audacious experimentation with polysemy, innovative use of words, forging of new lexemes and compounds, adept incorporation of foreign loans, dialectal and archaic forms, and breaking of traditional thought, it becomes a puzzle, a riddle, a task, and a game, all in one.

AFTERWORD III
THE STIGMATA OF WINGS: ON THE POETRY OF BOHDAN RUBCHAK

Mykola Riabchuk
(Translated by Michael M. Naydan)

Bohdan Rubchak isn't a political poet or, as we now call them in Ukraine, a "socially engaged" one. In all of his poems, we might try in vain to look for some direct "echoes" of "American reality" or, moreover, Ukrainian reality, which Rubchak gleaned only from reading the press until 1990 when he first visited Kyiv at the Golden Echo cultural festival. It was thought that he can't fathom all this reality (history, culture, and even language) other than in the form of "stigmata." Ukraine is present in his poetry only as a kind of potentiality, something that simultaneously exists and doesn't. It exists because of the Ukrainian language spoken by his parents, and he has a memory of "old yellowed magazines" and "train cars that long ago stopped humming," about "young boys who died" and "the girl who puts a mine underneath rails"; but it's absent – because you can't see that Ukraine anywhere in the world, and no ordinary American will tell you what it is and where it is, and the memory of a child is too feeble to hold a grain of first impressions under the pressure of a further, almost half-century of life experience in other places of paradise and in a different linguistic environment.

Certainly, therefore, in the poetry of Rubchak, as well as in the works of other poets of the Ukrainian diaspora, there is little concreteness, few vivid, unique details, fixed by a tenacious, "photographic" gaze. With Ukrainian features, everything is clear – it cannot be, ex nihilo nihil. But why does American realia not break through there – only "the smell of laundries, dirty restaurants," the "dust of sidewalks," "acanthus beds, sweaters, an attic," "a bit of snow and soot between stone walls," wind that "whips seagulls like old bits of newspapers," and even somewhere in the blink of an eye "sky, a cobblestone pavement, windows, a lamp"— although the poems sometimes have a very specific, underscored detailed name: "A Note from a Diary," "An Improvisation on the Fifteenth of November," "Several Observations," but we, in essence, will not find in his poetry those very observations (at least external, substantive ones, an American poetry that is so liberally inclined to a kind of "hyperrealism").

First of all we find a world of metaphors, a kind of "absolute reality," inhabited by creatures, mostly dull and often quite bizarre. Here you and the "dancers of trembling wills," and "aquarium of dreams," and the "abstraction of your body," and, finally, "the room – quadrilateral melancholy," as well as "on the surfaces of loneliness: the microagonies of microloving." One of its poles is the desire to go "to the farthest facets of life" – Rubchak's poetry definitely tends toward a poetics of surrealism – all the way to a purely philological game when the construction of the image is dictated mainly by the consonance of words, the logic of acoustical shaping, and not discourse per se ("I was furious, I was nuclear like a lamb, like a berry, like white fir, like a threshing-floor," or "like the fury of sage, like the enthrallment of wormwood"). But with its second pole, Rubchak's poetry nevertheless tends toward the narrative tradition, to depict a certain landscape of the soul, to quite rational thoughts and reflections:

> In restless sleep, tell me, whom you were looking for?
> Which peaceful day, whose hand?
> Which azure blue, which beneficial herbs,
> which God-given words that the years have not granted?
>
> Brothers reach the crowns and the blackest depths,
> they fly to plow the fields of the most distant worlds,
> but you don't accept these prideful hours,
> and your lips whisper: "That's not what I want from you."
>
> Cities circulate in veins, bridges shake in your eyes,
> mercilessly the grid of crossroads brands your brow,
> and the entire tenderness of the world, which you have never caressed,
> doesn't want to go away. It wounds with the blades of dreams. It hurts.

In a sense, this poem can be considered the program not only for Bohdan Rubchak but also for the entire generation of his peers, split between two worlds (and in two languages!) – between the "tenderness" of one world, which, in spite of everything, "wounds with the blades of dreams," and the cruelty, the "fossilization" of another, which nevertheless has its "crowns" and "depths" and which, after all, is the only or, at least, the most indescribable for the poet's reality.

I have already spoken about the pointlessness or, rather, the dearth of this reality. Language provides the strongest resistance to the surrounding American concrete realia, not, of course, in the vulgar understanding of the Ukrainian language, which it seems, is too poor to adequately reflect with its means all the fullness of foreign (and foreign-speaking) life – both material and spiritual (though certain, generally inescapable, problems, of course, arise here). The main problem is, as already has been noted, the psychological (and linguistic) duality of the poet: on the one hand – insufficient rootedness in the Ukrainian language and cultural environment (or, at least, the lack of a living, direct connection with it), and on the other – insufficient integration into the American environment (the lack of a complete identification with it, a certain linguistic and psychological detachment). The situation is dramatic in its own way: the American cosmic-psycho-logos rather weakly connects with the Ukrainian one; the matter, I emphasize once again, is not only so much in linguistic resources, but in the inadequacy of surrounding life (as a certain sum of spiritual acts in the context of a concrete civilization and its linguo-cultural conventions), and – the inner life of the poet, connected with a completely other civilization, its linguistic and cultural archetypes.

The simplest example consists of the "black poplars" and "poplars" that stubbornly crawl out of the American landscape in Rubchak's poetry. We do not question their authenticity, we also have no doubt that an American poet could have noticed and inserted these trees in his English-language verse, but we are sure that the American reader would not have given any meaningful significance to this particular detail, most likely, he would not have noticed it at all because, in his linguo-cultural tradition, "poplars" are simply "poplars," the trees of the same semantic series, as any others in his locality.

In this sense, national cosmic-psycho-logos are worlds whose inhabitants live in different light and sound ranges, and therefore they see and hear only a part of the foreign frequencies, and therefore they perceive a strange world, a stranger's being incomplete or, at least, not directly, but through some rational, conceptual devices.

In this regard, the "surrealism," or better, the "abstractness" of Rubchak's poetry is a phenomenon that to some extent is forced: it is not so much a consequence of a conscious establishment of "pointlessness," as a result of a peculiar "dream" existence between two worlds – the distant and nearly familiar, but native; and – the close and visible, but foreign. The primality of one is due to his or her forgotten to some degree nature and, as a result, to a certain mythic quality ("I am ... a little boy of those very own spring ... They are somewhere in another world ... In the memory of sleepy river reaches... In my mind"); the primality of another arises as a result of the author's linguistic and psychological resignation – a purely existentialist alienation is deepened by the alienation of the linguistic-national:

Trees swoon, weary,
cursed to a flood of glares,
by the wall of a dead city.

The cruel stone of thought
dishonors the youth of verdure,
maims the leaves of Aprils.

And the eternal tubers of roots
wind into primordial midnight
from rootless, bark-less days.

Beneath the pavement,
beneath homeless footsteps they search for
the promised land of a pine wood.

The "rootless" and "bark-less" being, mentioned by the author in the lines above, is a fairly precise metaphor for poetic alienation from both the past and the present. Each of these two aspects of poetry, taken separately, would look, if not trivial, in any case, not so interesting that we could talk about Rubchak's poetry as a completely original and unique phenomenon in modern Ukrainian literature. Together, in a peculiar synthesis, they form a truly unique and dramatic world, one that can be considered a kind of substitute or rather a common denominator of two real, equally (albeit for different reasons) impregnable/unapproachable worlds for the poet. In general, poetic intuition has rightly suggested to him that in these works these worlds can be connected, first of all, at the level of philosophical abstractions, eternal, "existential" concepts, metaphorical "concepts," and not at the level of subjective, verbal, emotional empiricism. This statement is already found in Rubchak's first poetry collection *The Garden of Stone* (1956), in the expressive programmatic poem "Ars poetica":

> To search only for the essence, to search for just the horizon of being –
> the essence of being. To feel space: the flight of black birds far off,
> to sense time: distinct drawings in black caves,
> and with an absolute wind to understand your day, poet.

A sense of the "Absolute," the ability to see phenomena and events not only in small but also in great, "cosmic" time and space gives Rubchak's creative works universal human significance, elevates them above the traditional (for diasporan poetry) groaning about historical misery, exile, "accursed roads," and at least traditional (not for diaspora poetry) quasi-existentialist sighs about the transitory nature of human life and the total absurdity of everything.

The surrounding petrification, which we find in Rubchak's poetry almost at every turn, is not an ontological quality of the world, but only a certain state of the human soul, the projection of this high rank. And that is why "depetrification" in principle is possible: all efforts of people, and even more so poets, should be directed toward this – to increase the orderliness of the universe and to reduce its entropy ("on stone branches," as Rubchak writes, "stone foliage has become green").

The disastrous times of people and even entire nations in this context are only partial manifestations of general entropy. Poets overcome it only by the only means at their disposal – the word, though it often resembles "harvest in December or the use of grapes in January." But the "stigmata of wings" appears in these newly formed Sisyphuses, which they seem to be "destined to be stuck in a dirty dresser like us" (like Saint-John Perse, just as T. S. Eliot, as well as dozens of other poets including Rubchak, who earned their daily bread by doing anything, just not with poetry). And Sisyphuses become Icaruses, it's in vain that "water awaits, the edge of a cliff awaits,"

> "No, you cannot stay here –
> you must get up and go."

Even if Rubchak's poetry was just one of many testimonies of how "it's difficult to hang forever as a bridge between two shores," then it would deserve our most rapt attention – ultimately both as an interesting human as well as a literary document. However, it seems to us, it also shows that it is difficult to hang not only between geographical, linguistic and cultural, ethnic "shores," but also between the shores of living, "existential" – between good and evil, intelligence and absurdity, life and death.

It is not necessary, in the end, to live in the Ukrainian diaspora to ask yourself the question: "Why do you live here? Your worlds have withered away..." – but one must still be a poet to answer it:

> But you're still waiting. Because at times
> a diaphanous bird arrives and calls you.
> With its wing it lights up your lips.

AFTERWORD IV
BOHDAN RUBCHAK (1935-2018): A CONCISE BIOGRAPHY

MICHAEL M. NAYDAN

On September 23, 2018 Bohdan Rubchak, a giant of Ukrainian poetry as well as of his fields of Ukrainian studies and comparative literature died at the age of 83. I vividly remember meeting Bohdan and his wife Mariana at the annual University of Illinois at Champaign-Urbana conferences in Ukrainian studies, which he and Ukrainian librarian Dmytro Shtohryn organized for many years. I attended the extraordinarily successful summer workshops in Ukrainian studies there several times, taking advantage of the university's amazing Slavic library collection as well as the great coffee shop a few blocks from the library where I would often meet with Ukrainian colleagues including Bohdan and Mariana.

The conference in 1991 was the largest in its history and was the first opportunity forme to interact with numerous younger Ukrainian writers and scholars, who had come thanks to funding from the Ukrainian Research Program, which Bohdan cofounded with Dmytro Shtohryn at the University of Illinois. Nearly a decade later my daughter and I translated several of Bohdan's poems for my *100 Years of Youth* anthology that I compiled with Olha Luchuk. I found his poetry to be emotional and refined with a plethora of literary and cultural allusions to works of classical and comparative literature that mirrored the depth and wide variety of his scholarly interests. Bohdan was an avid reader who kept informed about everything happening in Ukraine and actively interacted with numerous writers and scholars from there. He received an extremely positive reception as a poet in his homeland where he was treated with great respect by his new reading public. In evidence of that, he received the prestigious Pavlo Tychyna Prize for his poetry in 1993, two years after Ukrainian independence. He was also inducted into the Ukrainian Union of Writers.

Bohdan was very proud of the fact that he was born in the small city of Kalush, Ukraine in 1935. The city of about sixty thousand inhabitants is located in the foothills of the Carpathian Mountains. In 1943 eight-year-old Bohdan ended up in Kaufbeuren, Germany with his parents during the Nazi invasion of Western Ukraine. They were resettled in Dillingen, Germany in 1945 where the family moved in with a German family. His father died soon after in 1947, and he and his mother remained after the war in Germany until their emigration to the U.S. in 1948. Upon arrival in New York he soon moved with his mother to Chicago where he completed his high school education at Harrison Technical High School in 1953.

After high school, Bohdan matriculated at the University of Illinois at Navy Pier (a temporary branch of the university created to serve returning GIs) where he completed a two-year program, majoring in English with a minor in German. He published his first book of poetry *Kaminnyi sad* (The Stone Garden) in 1956. After the two-year program at the Navy Pier campus, he completed his B.A. degree at Roosevelt University in 1957 where he majored in English Literature with a minor in Philosophy. His further education was interrupted by a ten-month stint of military service in South Korea in 1958. His Korean tour of duty had been cut short at his mother's intervention.

Upon returning stateside Bohdan had his first major love affair, with a woman he calls Francesca in his poetry. The breakup with her caused him great emotional pain, which he documented in his second book of poetry *Promenysta zrada* (Radiant Betrayal; 1960). The new collection exhibited great philosophical depth and feeling in a mature and assured lyrical voice that became the hallmark of his poetry. He worked in the publishing field at The Commerce Clearing House from 1960-1962. During that time a close friendship with a woman from Chicago by the name of Oksana helped him overcome the deep emotional scars left by his relationship with Francesca, but vestiges of the pain remained with him long after. The collection *Divchyni bez krainy* (To the Girl without a Country), his third book of poetry, appeared in 1963. That same year, he earned an M.A. equivalent with a major in Russian literature from the University of Chicago. Bohdan then took a position as an Instructor at the University of Manitoba in 1963-1964 where he met his future wife Mariana. After marrying her in January 1965 he became part of a large instant family with Mariana's four young daughters from her first marriage.

Following the wedding, the family moved to Chicago where Bohdan worked at LaSalle Extension University until 1966. The following year they moved to the New York metropolitan area when Bohdan become the Director of the Ukrainian Desk of Radio Liberty in 1967. He published his fourth book of poetry, *Osobysta Klio* (A Personal Clio), in 1967, which was dedicated to Mariana. In 1969 he accepted a position at Rutgers University as an Instructor of Russian Language and Literature and taught there until 1973, while attending classes in comparative literature and working on his Ph.D. There he began to write his dissertation on an esoteric comparative literature topic under the title "Man is a Metaphor: Poetic Knowledge as Grounded in Perception, Imagination and Language," which he defended in 1977. He took a position at the University of Illinois at Chicago Circle (now known as just "at Chicago") in 1973, where he taught Ukrainian, Slavic, and comparative literature until his retirement in 2005.

His brief collection *Marenu topyty* (To Drown Marena) was written in 1980 as part of his selected works edition *Krylo Ikarove* (The Wing of Icarus) and appeared in 1983. There is some confusion about this date. He wrote in his diary in 1981 that he was rushing to complete it so that it could be published before the end of the year. It was republished in newly independent Ukraine in 1991 in an expanded edition with some newly penned poems. He stopped writing and publishing his poetry following that sixth collection. After his retirement, he and his wife Mariana, a professor of history at Valparaiso University, retired to Boonton, New Jersey, to be closer to family.

Bohdan's poetic sensibility was shaped by his membership in the New York Group of Ukrainian poets, which arose in the mid-1950s. Besides Bohdan, the initial members of the group included Bohdan Boychuk, Yuri Tarnawsky, Patricia Kylyna (now better known as Patricia Nell Warren), Emma Andijewska, Zhenia Vasylkivska, and Vira Vovk. Their youthful energy, their love of poetry, the common émigré experience of growing up as bicultural, bilingual Ukrainians in a foreign land, their personal friendships, and common Western literary influences united them. They, however, were less of a literary movement or school per se and more of a group (as their name denotes) of like-minded friends with lofty literary tastes and talents. Bohdan published over 300 poems during his lifetime. His scholarly writings consisted of more than 30 articles, over 20 chapters and introductions in books, and more than 30 minor articles and reviews. His essays, mostly written in Ukrainian, are all thoughtful and thought-provoking and wide-ranging in scope.

Besides writings on his fellow New York Group poets and individual writers such as Taras Shevchenko, Bohdan Ihor Antonych, Bohdan Kravtsiv, Evhen Malaniuk, Vasyl Barka, Vasyl Makhno, and many others, topics of his essays included experimental Ukrainian poetry, contemporary American poetry, Ukrainian Modernism, new Ukrainian poets of the 1980s and 1990s, and the philosophy of Gaston Bachelard. I consider his annotations of and lengthy introduction to Marco Carynnyk's translation of Mykhailo Kotsiubynsky's Shadows of Forgotten Ancestors (Ukrainian Academic Press, 1981) a must read for Ukrainianists and a brilliantly researched analysis of indigenous Carpathian folklore upon which Kotsyubynsky based his famous novella. It was published under the title "The Music of Satan and the Bedeviled World: An Essay on Mykhailo Kotsyubynsky."

Anthologizing Ukrainian poetry in the diaspora comprised one of the most passionate areas of Bohdan's publication activity. With Bohdan Boychuk he compiled and co-edited the handsome two-volume collection of émigré Ukrainian poetry *Koordynaty: antolohiia suchasnoi ukrainskoi poezii na zakhodi* (Coordinates: An Anthology of Contemporary Ukrainian Poetry in the West) [Suchasnist Publishers, 1969]. It included biocritical sketches of all the poets penned by the two Bohdans as well as a critical introduction by John Fizer.

He was on the editorial board of the prominent Ukrainian journal Suchasnist from 1962 when it was based in Munich and New York nearly until it moved back to Kyiv, Ukraine after independence in 1991. He served on the editorial board of several other journals including Journal of Ukrainian Studies, Harvard Ukrainian Studies, Slovo, and Svito-vyd. He often refereed articles for major North American Slavic journals including Slavic Review, Slavic and East European Journal, and Canadian Slavonic Papers. Besides his poetry written in Ukrainian along with literary criticism, he also wrote 30 poems in English and translated poetry from other languages (mostly French) into English.

His collected literary essays appeared in Ukrainian in Vasyl Gabor's Private Collection series with Piramida Publishers in Lviv, Ukraine in 2012 under the title *Mity metamorfoz, abo poshuky dobroho svitu: esei* (Myths of Metamorphoses, or In Search of a Good World: Essays).

In 2016 his short stories were published by Vasyl Gabor in his Pryvatna kolektsiia series under the title Bohdan Rubchak. Most recently with his close friend Bohdan Boychuk and Eleonora Solovey he published a bilingual edition of translations of twentieth-century Ukrainian poet Volodymyr Svidzinsky's poetry under the title *Evasive Shadow of Life: Selected Poems* (Canadian Institute of Ukrainian Studies, 2017). He kept actively working despite increasing infirmity nearly to the very end of his life. He was taken to intensive care on September 18, 2018 and died on September 23 five days later.

AFTERWORD V
TIMELINE OF BOHDAN RUBCHAK (1935-2018)

1935 Born March 6 in Kalush, Ukraine

1943 Emigrated to Germany during the World War II with his father and mother. First settled in the city of Kaufbeuren in a Displaced Persons camp.

1945 Resettled in Dillingen, Germany

1947 Death of father in Dillingen

1948 Emigrated with mother to New York City and shortly after arrival moved to Chicago

1953 Completed Harrison Technical High School in Chicago and began a two-year program of studies at the University of Illinois at Navy Pier (now called the U. of Illinois at Chicago)

1956 Published first collection of poetry *The Stone Garden (Kaminnyi sad)*, which can also be translated as *The Stone Orchard*

1957 Completed his BA degree at Roosevelt University in 1957 with a major in English Literature and a minor in Philosophy

1958 Signed up for a two-year tour of duty in Korea that was cut short by his mother's intervention and returned to the U.S. after a year

1958-1960 Love affair with Francesca

1960 Published second book of poetry *The Radiant Betrayal*

1960-1962 Worked at The Commerce Clearing House

1961-1963 Close friendship with Oksana

1962-1965 Attended the University of Chicago Graduate School with a major in Russian literature, earning an M.A. equivalent

1963 Moved to Canada to teach at the University of Manitoba where he met wife-to-be Mariana in September

1964 In the summer and fall moved back to Chicago at his mother's demand for a temporary stay

1964 Published several short stories in the then émigré journal Suchasnist

1965 Returned to Winnipeg after the New Year and married Mariana on January 22, 1965. Moved back to Chicago with Mariana and her four daughters from her first marriage

1965-1966 Worked at LaSalle Extension University

1967 Moved to Forest Hills, NY with family. Began work at Radio Liberty Ukrainian Division. Assigned for two months to the Radio Liberty office in Munich but returned after one month. Upon returning began a close friendship with two prominent Soviet-period poets from Ukraine – Ivan Drach and Dmytro Pavlychko

1967 Published his fourth collection with a dedication to his wife Mariana *A Personal Clio*, which was reissued with a new cover design almost immediately

1969 Moved to New Brunswick, New Jersey where he began graduate school in Comparative Literature at Rutgers University and taught Russian literature

1971 Wife Mariana received Phi Beta Kappa B.A. degree in History from Douglass College

1973 Wife Mariana received M.A. degree in Intellectual History from Rutgers

1973 Passed his Ph.D. oral exams

1973 Moved to Chicago where he began working as an Assistant Professor at U. of Illinois at Chicago in the Department of Slavic Languages and Literature

1975 Turned 40, precipitating a mid-life crisis that lasted thirteen years until 1988

1977 Defended his dissertation titled "Man is a Metaphor: Poetic Knowledge as Grounded in Perception, Imagination and Language"

1983 Published fifth collection *Drowning Marena* as part of his selected poetry edition *The Wing of Icarus*

1988 Wife Mariana defended her dissertation. Began tenure-track appointment following two years as a part-time replacement at Valparaiso University.

1991 Published his final expanded selected poetry edition *The Wing of Icarus* in newly independent Ukraine

1993 Received the Pavlo Tychyna Prize in poetry. Traveled to Ukraine with Mariana to receive it. During the trip his mother hospitalized at age 88 after a fall and later in November that year placed in a nursing home after staying for several weeks with Bohdan and Mariana.

1995 Following a brain operation, mother was left comatose and remained in that state under nursing care for five years

2000 Mother's death

2005 Retired from teaching and moved to Boonton, New Jersey

2006 Mariana moved to Boonton after her retirement and received a nine-year appointment as a Senior Research Professor off site

2011 Attended final public function – Mariana's eightieth birthday celebration at Shevchenko Scientific Society in New York City

2012 Published a collection of his literary essays in Ukrainian *Mity metamorfoz, abo poshuky dobroho svitu: esei*(Myths of Metamorphoses, or In Search of a Good World: Essays) in Lviv, Ukraine (Pryvatna koletkstia of Piramida Publishers, Vasyl Gabor, ed.)

2016 Short stories published by Vasyl Gabor in his Privatna kolektsiia series under the title *Bohdan Rubchak*

2017 With Bohdan Boychuk and Eleonora Solovey published a bilingual edition of translations of twentieth-century Ukrainian poet Volodymyr Svidzinsky's poetry under the title *Evasive Shadow of Life: Selected Poems* (Canadian Institute of Ukrainian Studies)

2018 Taken to intensive care on September 18 and died on September 23 in the hospital

AFTERWORD VI
PAGE NUMBERS OF PUBLICATIONS WHERE POEMS FIRST APPEARED

The number in parentheses following the title of each poem indicates the page number of the original Ukrainian version found in the selected poetry edition The Wing of Icarus (Krylo Ikarove) *published in Ukraine in 1991. For poems not appearing there, the page number with an asterisk designate the original edition in which it first appeared.*

from the collection THE STONE GARDEN (1956)
    "In a room of a hundred mirrors…" (p. 164)
    AUTUMN (p. 7*)
    "The lips of leaves…" (p. 8*)
    "The graves of my great grandsons were here…" (p. 9*)
    TO HAMLET (p. 23*)
    NOCTURNAL MINIATURES (p. 167)
    MIDNIGHT IMPROVISATION (p. 187)
    ARS POETICA (p. 191)
    FROM THE SONG OF SONGS (p. 195-197)

from the collection THE RADIANT BETRAYAL (1960)
    THE RADIANT BETRAYAL (p. 126)
    FOR FRANCESCA (p. 132)
    FOR FRANCESCA AGAIN (p. 133)
    THE ANGEL'S BETRAYAL (p. 134)

NOVEMBER (p. 14*)
DECEMBER (p. 15*)
A RECOLLECTION OF THE MOON (p. 139)
THE WING OF ICARUS (p. 153-4)
BE SILENT (p. 155)

arom the collection *TO THE GIRL WITHOUT A COUNTRY* (1963)

TO THE GIRL WITHOUT A COUNTRY (p. 96)
AND THEN WE RODE HOME (p. 7*)
A SLEEPLESS NIGHT (p. 99)
FROM GOTTRIED BENN (p. 100)
THE DANCER (p. 101)
SONG OF A WOMAN BENEATH THE MOON (p. 102)
IN THE LAST HOUSE OF THE MIRROR (p. 16*)
ABSENCE (p. 17*)
THREE EMBLEMS (p. 103-104)
THE FARNESS OF ROADS (p. 105)
A WINDY ICARUS (p. 108)
A RESTLESS SLEEP (p. 111)
THE DESTINATION (p. 116)
AN AUTUMN DAY (p.118)

from the collection *A PERSONAL CLIO* (1967)
AN AUTUMN ROMANCE (p. 28-29*)
TO CLIO (p. 66)
THREE FRAGMENTS OF "THE WORD" (p. 67-68)
A STONE (p. 69)
DON JUAN (p. 72)
MOZART (p. 76)
CHOPIN (pp. 77-8)
A SMALL POET (p. 80)
MY ITHACA (p. 81)
A WINTRY ROMANCE (p. 83)
A SONG FOR MARIANA (p. 89)
NOTES FROM A DIARY (p. 89-91)
    1. THE FIRST POEM
    2. OUTSIDE THE WINDOW

3. A JUSTIFICATION
4. SEVERAL OBSERVATIONS

From the collection *DROWNING MARENA* (1980)
DROWNING MARENA (p. 36)
A LETTER TO HOME (p. 50)
A BOOK FROM HOME (p. 51)
DECADENCE (p. 52)
A FLASH AND A REFLECTION (p. 53)
A MANDARIN FOR MY WIFE (p. 56)
THE FEMALE SAINT AND THE DEVIL (p. 57)
SKETCHES (p. 61-62)
    1. A MADRIGAL
    2. COMPLAINING ABOUT DECEMBER
THE GODS (From W.S. Merwin) (p. 64)

from the collection *THE WING OF ICARUS* (1983; 1991)
THE BLACKSMITH (p. 18)
RAIN (p. 19)
AN EVENING PRAYER (p. 20)
NARCISSUS (p. 21)
THE HARDEST GAME (p. 22)
DRAMATURGY (p. 23)
COMPRESSIONS (p. 24-26)

SEVEN SIGNS OF THE LION
by Michael M. Naydan

The novel *Seven Signs of the Lion* is a magical journey to the city of Lviv in Western Ukraine. Part magical realism, part travelogue, part adventure novel, and part love story, it is a fragmented, hybrid work about a mysterious and mythical place. The hero of the novel Nicholas Bilanchuk is a gatherer of living souls, the unique individuals he meets over the course of his five-month stay in his ancestral homeland. These include the enigmatic Mr. Viktor, who, with one eye that always glimmers, in a dream summons him across the Atlantic Ocean to the city of lions, becoming his spiritual mentor; the genius mathematician Professor Potojbichny (a man of science with a mystical bent and whose name means "man from the other side"); the exquisite beauty Ada, whose name suggests "woman from Hades" in Ukrainian, whose being emanates irresistible sensuality, but who never lets anyone capture her beauty in a picture; the schizophrenic artist Ivan the Ghostseer, who lives in a bohemian hovel of a basement apartment and in an alcohol-induced trance paints the spirits of the city that torment him; and the curly-haired elfin Raya, whose name suggests "paradise" in Ukrainian and who becomes the primary guide and companion for Nicholas on his journey to self-realization...

Buy it > www.glagoslav.com

HERSTORIES: AN ANTHOLOGY OF NEW UKRAINIAN WOMEN PROSE WRITERS

Women's prose writing has exploded on the literary scene in Ukraine just prior to and following Ukrainian independence in 1991. Over the past two decades scores of fascinating new women authors have emerged. These authors write in a wide variety of styles and genres including short stories, novels, essays, and new journalism. In the collection you will find: realism, magical realism, surrealism, the fantastic, deeply intellectual writing, newly discovered feminist perspectives, philosophical prose, psychological mysteries, confessional prose, and much more.

The volume will include 18 contemporary writers: Lina Kostenko, Emma Andijewska, Nina Bichuya, Sofia Maidanska, Ludmyla Taran, Liuko Dashvar, Maria Matios, Eugenia Kononenko, Oksana Zabuzhko, Iren Rozdobudko, Natalka Sniadanko, Larysa Denysenko, Svitlana Povaljajeva, Svitlana Pyrkalo, Dzvinka Matiash, Irena Karpa, Tanya Malyarchuk, and Sofia Andrukhovych.

Buy it > www.glagoslav.com

Contours of the City
by Attyla Mohylny

Contours of the City arguably comprises one of the finest collections of free verse ever written in Ukrainian even though it was largely overlooked when it first appeared during the political transition to Ukrainian independence in 1991. It certainly deserves a broader audience both in Mohylny's homeland as well as in the wider world. While it may be described as a one-hit wonder because of the poet's premature death, it remains a brilliant hit for all time.

Translator Michael Naydan received the Eugene Kayden Meritorious Achievement Award in Translation from the University of Colorado for a partial manuscript of his translations of Mohylny's poetry into English in 1993. This edition includes a complete translation of Mohylny's collection *Contours of the City* along with several poems translated by Virlana Tkacz and Wanda Phipps.

Buy it > www.glagoslav.com

CONVERSATIONS BEFORE SILENCE:

THE SELECTED POETRY OF OLES ILCHENKO

An avid reader of English-language poets such as William Carlos Williams and Stanley Kunitz, Ilchenko is one of the best Ukrainian poets writing in free verse today. His poetry is associative, flitting, and fragmentary. At times he does not form complete sentences in his poems and links words together into phrases before shifting into another thought or idea. The language of his poetry has a tendency to collapse into itself, often forcing the reader to reevaluate a word or line, to reread a previous word to focus on the poet's inner logic. This fragmentary incompleteness and permeability mimics much the way human consciousness works without the filter of the written communicative convention of sentences and grammatical structure. This "slipperiness" and rapid shifting of voice comprises one of the essential invariants in Ilchenko's poetics. The poet also flaunts many traditional poetic Ukrainian conventions. Like ee cummings he tends to avoid capital letters or punctuation such as exclamation points. One will find only commas and dashes for pauses, and an occasional period in his poems, which do not always end with the finality of that punctuation mark...

Buy it > www.glagoslav.com

Dear Reader,

Thank you for purchasing this book.

We at Glagoslav Publications are glad to welcome you, and hope that you find our books to be a source of knowledge and inspiration.

We want to show the beauty and depth of the Slavic region to everyone looking to expand their horizon and learn something new about different cultures, different people, and we believe that with this book we have managed to do just that.

Now that you've got to know us, we want to get to know you. We value communication with our readers and want to hear from you! We offer several options:

— Join our Book Club on Goodreads, Library Thing and Shelfari, and receive special offers and information about our giveaways;

— Share your opinion about our books on Amazon, Barnes & Noble, Waterstones and other bookstores;

— Join us on Facebook and Twitter for updates on our publications and news about our authors;

— Visit our site www.glagoslav.com to check out our Catalogue and subscribe to our Newsletter.

Glagoslav Publications is getting ready to release a new collection and planning some interesting surprises — stay with us to find out!

Glagoslav Publications
Email: contact@glagoslav.com

Glagoslav Publications Catalogue

- *The Time of Women* by Elena Chizhova
- *Andrei Tarkovsky: The Collector of Dreams* by Layla Alexander-Garrett
- *Andrei Tarkovsky - A Life on the Cross* by Lyudmila Boyadzhieva
- *Sin* by Zakhar Prilepin
- *Hardly Ever Otherwise* by Maria Matios
- *Khatyn* by Ales Adamovich
- *The Lost Button* by Irene Rozdobudko
- *Christened with Crosses* by Eduard Kochergin
- *The Vital Needs of the Dead* by Igor Sakhnovsky
- *The Sarabande of Sara's Band* by Larysa Denysenko
- *A Poet and Bin Laden* by Hamid Ismailov
- *Watching The Russians (Dutch Edition)* by Maria Konyukova
- *Kobzar* by Taras Shevchenko
- *The Stone Bridge* by Alexander Terekhov
- *Moryak* by Lee Mandel
- *King Stakh's Wild Hunt* by Uladzimir Karatkevich
- *The Hawks of Peace* by Dmitry Rogozin
- *Harlequin's Costume* by Leonid Yuzefovich
- *Depeche Mode* by Serhii Zhadan
- *The Grand Slam and other stories (Dutch Edition)* by Leonid Andreev
- *METRO 2033 (Dutch Edition)* by Dmitry Glukhovsky
- *METRO 2034 (Dutch Edition)* by Dmitry Glukhovsky
- *A Russian Story* by Eugenia Kononenko
- *Herstories, An Anthology of New Ukrainian Women Prose Writers*
- *The Battle of the Sexes Russian Style* by Nadezhda Ptushkina
- *A Book Without Photographs* by Sergey Shargunov
- *Down Among The Fishes* by Natalka Babina
- *disUNITY* by Anatoly Kudryavitsky
- *Sankya* by Zakhar Prilepin
- *Wolf Messing* by Tatiana Lungin
- *Good Stalin* by Victor Erofeyev
- *Solar Plexus* by Rustam Ibragimbekov
- *Don't Call me a Victim!* by Dina Yafasova
- *Poetin (Dutch Edition)* by Chris Hutchins and Alexander Korobko
- *A History of Belarus* by Lubov Bazan

- *Children's Fashion of the Russian Empire* by Alexander Vasiliev
- *Empire of Corruption - The Russian National Pastime* by Vladimir Soloviev
- *Heroes of the 90s: People and Money. The Modern History of Russian Capitalism*
- *Fifty Highlights from the Russian Literature (Dutch Edition)* by Maarten Tengbergen
- *Bajesvolk (Dutch Edition)* by Mikhail Khodorkovsky
- *Tsarina Alexandra's Diary (Dutch Edition)*
- *Myths about Russia* by Vladimir Medinskiy
- *Boris Yeltsin: The Decade that Shook the World* by Boris Minaev
- *A Man Of Change: A study of the political life of Boris Yeltsin*
- *Sberbank: The Rebirth of Russia's Financial Giant* by Evgeny Karasyuk
- *To Get Ukraine* by Oleksandr Shyshko
- *Asystole* by Oleg Pavlov
- *Gnedich* by Maria Rybakova
- *Marina Tsvetaeva: The Essential Poetry*
- *Multiple Personalities* by Tatyana Shcherbina
- *The Investigator* by Margarita Khemlin
- *The Exile* by Zinaida Tulub
- *Leo Tolstoy: Flight from paradise* by Pavel Basinsky
- *Moscow in the 1930* by Natalia Gromova
- *Laurus (Dutch edition)* by Evgenij Vodolazkin
- *Prisoner* by Anna Nemzer
- *The Crime of Chernobyl: The Nuclear Goulag* by Wladimir Tchertkoff
- *Alpine Ballad* by Vasil Bykau
- *The Complete Correspondence of Hryhory Skovoroda*
- *The Tale of Aypi* by Ak Welsapar
- *Selected Poems* by Lydia Grigorieva
- *The Fantastic Worlds of Yuri Vynnychuk*
- *The Garden of Divine Songs and Collected Poetry of Hryhory Skovoroda*
- *Adventures in the Slavic Kitchen: A Book of Essays with Recipes*
- *Seven Signs of the Lion* by Michael M. Naydan
- *Forefathers' Eve* by Adam Mickiewicz
- *One-Two* by Igor Eliseev

- *Girls, be Good* by Bojan Babić
- *Time of the Octopus* by Anatoly Kucherena
- *The Grand Harmony* by Bohdan Ihor Antonych
- *The Selected Lyric Poetry Of Maksym Rylsky*
- *The Shining Light* by Galymkair Mutanov
- *The Frontier: 28 Contemporary Ukrainian Poets - An Anthology*
- *Acropolis: The Wawel Plays* by Stanisław Wyspiański
- *Contours of the City* by Attyla Mohylny
- *Conversations Before Silence: The Selected Poetry of Oles Ilchenko*
- *The Secret History of my Sojourn in Russia* by Jaroslav Hašek
- *Mirror Sand: An Anthology of Russian Short Poems*
- *Maybe We're Leaving* by Jan Balaban
- *Death of the Snake Catcher* by Ak Welsapar
- *A Brown Man in Russia* by Vijay Menon
- *Hard Times* by Ostap Vyshnia
- *The Flying Dutchman* by Anatoly Kudryavitsky
- *Nikolai Gumilev's Africa* by Nikolai Gumilev
- *Combustions* by Srđan Srdić
- *The Sonnets* by Adam Mickiewicz
- *Dramatic Works* by Zygmunt Krasiński
- *Four Plays* by Juliusz Słowacki
- *Little Zinnobers* by Elena Chizhova
- *We Are Building Capitalism! Moscow in Transition 1992-1997*
- *The Nuremberg Trials* by Alexander Zvyagintsev
- *The Hemingway Game* by Evgeni Grishkovets
- *A Flame Out at Sea* by Dmitry Novikov
- *Jesus' Cat* by Grig
- *Want a Baby and Other Plays* by Sergei Tretyakov
- *I Mikhail Bulgakov: The Life and Times* by Marietta Chudakova
- *Leonardo's Handwriting* by Dina Rubina
- *A Burglar of the Better Sort* by Tytus Czyżewski
- *The Mouseiad and other Mock Epics* by Ignacy Krasicki
- *Ravens before Noah* by Susanna Harutyunyan
- *Duel* by Borys Antonenko-Davydovych
- *An English Queen and Stalingrad* by Natalia Kulishenko
- *Point Zero* by Narek Malian
- *Absolute Zero* by Artem Chekh
- *Olanda* by Rafał Wojasiński
- *Robinsons* by Aram Pachyan
- *The Monastery* by Zakhar Prilepin

www.ingramcontent.com/pod-product-compliance
Lightning Source LLC
Chambersburg PA
CBHW021437080526
44588CB00009B/572